THE C

40 Daily Devotional Readings On The
Crucifixion Of Christ

Charles H. Spurgeon

justworshipgod.com

For a free ebook, more resources to help everybody apply the good news of Jesus to everyday life, and to be the first to hear about our latest releases and special offers, visit justworshipgod.com

Find us everywhere on social media @justworshipgod

Contents

Introduction

"We have often read the story of our Saviour's sufferings; but we cannot read it too often" said Charles Spurgeon as he opened his Bible to Luke's account of the crucifixion, "Let us, therefore, once again return to the place called Calvary".

Take 10 minutes each day and let Spurgeon warm your heart with joy that can only be found in the good news of Jesus Christ.

The Prince of Preachers examines the atonement with rich imagery and penetrating insight on the journey to Golgotha and Jesus' cries from the cross. Morning or evening, fill your mind with meditation on Jesus' death in your place.

These daily devotional readings have been taken from a selection of Spurgeon's sermons on the cross and the language has been updated for the modern reader. For more of Spurgeon's sermons, we recommend

http://www.spurgeon.org/index/rindex.php

1 – The Procession of Sorrow

So they took Jesus, and he went out, bearing his own cross

(John 19:16 ESV)

After our Lord Jesus Christ had been formally condemned by Pilate, our text tells us he was led away. Pilate scourged our Saviour according to the common custom of Roman courts. The soldiers executed their cruel office upon his shoulders with their rods and scourges, until the stripes had reached the full number. Jesus is formally condemned to crucifixion, but before he is led away he is given over to the Praetorian guards that those rough legionaries may insult him.

They mocked and insulted him in every way that cruelty and scorn could devise. The platted crown of thorns, the purple robe, the reed with which they struck him, and the spittle with which they disfigured him, all these marked the contempt in which they held the King of the Jews. When they had mocked him they pulled off the purple garment he had worn, this rough operation would cause much pain. His wounds untreated and raw, fresh bleeding from beneath the lash, would make this scarlet robe adhere to him, and when it was dragged off; his gashes would bleed anew.

He went forth carrying his cross upon his shoulders. This was intended at once to proclaim his guilt and intimate his doom. Usually the crier went before with an announcement such as this, "This is Jesus of Nazareth, King of the Jews, who for making himself a King, and stirring up the people, has been condemned to die."

This cross was a ponderous machine; not so heavy, perhaps, as some pictures would represent it, but still no light burden to a man whose shoulders were raw with the lashes of the Roman scourge. He had been all night in agony, he had spent the early morning at the hall of Caiaphas, he had been hurried, as I described to you last Sunday, from Caiaphas to Pilate, from Pilate to Herod, and from Herod back again to Pilate; he had, therefore, but little strength left, and you will not wonder that we find him staggering beneath his load, and that another is called to bear it with him. He goes forth, then, bearing his cross.

What do we learn as we see Christ led forth? Do we not see here the truth of that which was set forth in shadow by *the scape-goat?* Did not the high-priest bring the scape-goat, and put both his hands upon its head, confessing the sins of the people, that thus those sins might be laid upon the goat? Then the goat was led away by a fit man into the wilderness, and it carried away the sins of the people, so that if they were sought for, they could not be found.

Now we see Jesus brought before the priests and rulers, who pronounce him guilty; God himself imputes our sins *to him;* he was made sin for us; and, as the substitute for our guilt, bearing our sin upon his shoulders — for that cross was a sort of representation in wood of our guilt and doom — we see the great Scape-goat led away by the appointed officers of justice. Bearing upon his back the sin of all his people, the offering goes without the camp.

Beloved, can you say he carried *your* sin? As you look at the cross upon his shoulders does it represent *your* sin? Oh I raise the question, and be not satisfied unless you can answer it most positively in the affirmative.

There is one way by which you can tell whether he carried your sin or not. Have you laid your hand upon his head, confessed your sin, and trusted in him? Then your sin lies not on you; not one single ounce or drachma of it lies on you; it has all been transferred by blessed imputation to Christ, and he bears it on his shoulder in the form of yonder heavy cross.

What joy, what satisfaction this will give if we can sing—

"My soul looks back to see
The burden you didst bear,
When hanging to the accursed tree,
And knows her guilt was there!"[1]

---

[1] Not all the blood of beasts, Isaac Watts

Do not let the picture vanish till you have satisfied yourselves once for all that Christ was here the substitute for you.[2]

---

[2] The Procession of Sorrow – Sermon delivered March 1st 1863

2 – Outside the Camp

So they took Jesus, and he went out, bearing his own cross

(John 19:16 ESV)

Let us muse upon the fact that Jesus was conducted outside the gates of the city. It was the common place of death. That little rising ground, which was called Golgotha, the place of a skull, from its somewhat resembling the crown of a man's skull, was the common place of execution. It was one of Death's castles; here he stored his gloomiest trophies; he was the grim lord of that stronghold. Our great hero, the destroyer of Death, bearded the lion in his den, slew the monster in his own castle, and dragged the dragon captive from his own den.

I imagine Death thought it a splendid triumph when he saw the Master impaled and bleeding in the dominions of destruction; little did he know that the grave was to be rifled, and himself destroyed, by that crucified Son of man.

Calvary was the usual place of execution for the district. Christ must die a felon's death, and it must be upon the felon's gallows, in the place where horrid crimes had met their due reward. This added to his shame; but, in this, too, he draws the nearer to us, "He was numbered with the transgressors, and bore the sin of many, and made intercession for the transgressors."[3]

This, I think, is the great lesson from Christ's being slaughtered without the gate of the city — "let us go forth, therefore, outside the camp, bearing his reproach"[4] You see there the crowd are leading him forth from the temple. He is not allowed to worship with them. The ceremonial of the Jewish religion denies him any participation in its rituals; the priests condemn him never again to tread the hallowed floors, never again to look upon the consecrated altars in the place of his people's worship.

---

[3] Isaiah 53:12
[4] Hebrews 13:3

He is exiled from their friendship, too. No man dare call him friend now, or whisper a word of comfort to him. He is banished from their society, as if he were a leper whose breath would be infectious and whose presence would scatter plague. They force him outside the walls, and are not satisfied till they have rid themselves of his obnoxious presence.

For him they have no tolerance. Barabbas may go free; the thief and the murderer may be spared; but for Christ there is no word, but "Away with such a fellow from the earth! It is not fit that he should live." Jesus is therefore hunted out of the city.

Here is a picture of what we may expect from men if we are faithful to our Master. It is not likely that we shall be able to worship with their worship. They prefer a pompous ceremony; the swell of music, the glitter of costly garments, the parade of grandeur, and thus shut out the simple followers of the Lamb. The high places of earth's worship and honour are not for us. If we be true to our Master we shall soon lose the friendship of the world. The sinful find our conversation distasteful; in our pursuits the carnal have no interest; things dear to us are dross to worldlings, while things precious to them are contemptible to us.

There have been times, and the days may come again, when faithfulness to Christ has entailed exclusion from what is called "society." The world has in former days counted it God's service to kill the saints. If we would cleave more closely to Christ we might expect to receive more slander, more abuse, less tolerance, and less favour from men.

Oh! You Christians, who dream of trimming your sails to the wind, who seek to win the world's favour, I beseech you cease from a course so perilous. We are in the world, but we must never be of it; we are not to be secluded like monks in the cloister, but we are to be separated like Jews among Gentiles; men, but not of men; helping, aiding, befriending, teaching, comforting, instructing, but not sinning either to escape a frown or to win a smile.

The more obvious the great gulf between the Church and the world, the better shall it be for both; the better for the world, for it shall be warned; and the better for the Church, for it shall be preserved. Go, then, like the Master, expecting to be abused, to wear an ill-name, and to earn reproach; go you, like him, outside the camp.[5]

---

[5] The Procession of Sorrow – Sermon delivered March 1st 1863

3 – Carrying His Cross

So they took Jesus, and he went out, bearing his own cross

(John 19:16 ESV)

Let us now gaze for a while upon Christ carrying his cross.

Christ comes forth from Pilate's hall with the cumbrous wood upon his shoulder, but through weariness he travels slowly, and his enemies urgent for his death, and half afraid, from his emaciated appearance, that he may die before he reaches the place of execution, allow another to carry his burden. They place the cross upon Simon, a Cyrenian, coming out of the country. We are not sure that Simon was a disciple of Christ; he may have been a friendly spectator. Coming fresh from the country, not knowing what was going on, he joined with the mob, and they made him carry the cross. Whether a disciple then or not, we have every reason to believe that he became so afterwards; he was the father, we read, of Alexander and Rufus, two persons who appear to have been well known in the early Church; let us hope that salvation came to his house when he was compelled to bear the Saviour's cross.

Dear friends, we must remember that, although no one died on the cross with Christ, for atonement must be executed by a solitary Saviour, another person did carry the cross for Christ; for this world, while redeemed by price by Christ, and by Christ alone, is to be redeemed by divine power manifested in the sufferings and labours of the saints as well as those of Christ.

The ransom of men was all paid by Christ; that was redemption by price. But power is wanted to dash down those idols, to overcome the hosts of error; where is it to be found? In the Lord of Hosts, who shows his power in the sufferings of Christ and of his Church. The Church must suffer, that the gospel may be spread by her means. This is what the Apostle meant when he said, "I fill up that which is behind of the afflictions of Christ in my flesh for his body's sake, which is the Church."[6]

---

[6] Colossians 1:24

We see in Simon's carrying the cross a picture of what the Church is to do throughout all generations. Mark then, Christian, Jesus does not suffer so as to exclude your suffering. He bears a cross, not that you may escape it, but that you may endure it. Christ does exempt you from sin, but not from sorrow; he does take the curse of the cross, but he does not take the cross of the curse away from you. Remember that, and expect to suffer.

Beloved, let us comfort ourselves with this thought, that in our case, as in Simon's, it is not our cross, but Christ's cross which we carry. When your religion brings the trial of cruel mockings upon you; then remember, it is not your cross, it is Christ's cross; and how delightful is it to carry the cross of our Lord Jesus?

You carry the cross after him. You have blessed company; your path is marked with footprints of your Lord. If you will look, there is the mark of his blood-red shoulder upon that heavy cross. It is his cross, and he goes before you as a shepherd goes before his sheep. Take up your cross daily and follow him.

Although Simon carried Christ's cross, he did not volunteer to do it, but they compelled him. I fear me, beloved, I fear me that the most of us if we ever do carry it, carry it by compulsion, at least when it first comes on to our shoulders we do not like it, and would fain run from it, but the world compels us to bear Christ's cross. Cheerfully accept this burden, you servants of the Lord. I do not think we should seek after needless persecution. That man is a fool and deserves no pity, who purposely excites the disgust of other people. No, no; we must not make a cross of our own. Let there be nothing but your religion to object to, and then if that offends them let them be offended, it is a cross which you must carry joyfully.

Well, beloved, the cross we have to carry is only for a little while at most. A few times the sun will go up and down the hill; a few more moons will wax and wane, and then we shall receive the glory. "I consider that these light afflictions, which are but for a moment, are not worthy to be compared with the glory which shall be revealed in us."[7] We should love the cross, and count it very dear, because it works out for us a far more exceeding and eternal weight of glory. Christians, will you refuse to be cross-bearers for Christ?

Take up your cross, and go outside the camp, following your Lord, even until death.[8]

---

[7] 2 Corinthians 4:17
[8] The Procession of Sorrow – Sermon delivered March 1st 1863

4 - Sympathy

So they took Jesus, and he went out, bearing his own cross

(John 19:16 ESV)

As Christ went through the streets, a great multitude looked on. In the crowd there was a sparse sprinkling of tender-hearted women, probably those who had been healed, or whose children had been blessed by him. They raised an exceeding loud and bitter cry,ᵗ like Rachel weeping for her children, who would not be comforted, because they were not. The voice of sympathy prevailed over the voice of scorn.

Jesus paused, and said, "Daughters of Jerusalem, weep not for me; but weep for yourselves and for your children."[9] The sorrow of these good women was a very proper sorrow; Jesus did not by any means forbid it, he only recommended another sorrow as being better.

---

[9] Luke 23:28

The most scriptural way to describe the sufferings of Christ is not by labouring to excite sympathy through highly-coloured descriptions of his blood and wounds. What, then, dear friends, should be the sorrows excited by a view of Christ's sufferings? They are these—Weep not because the Savior bled, but because your sins made him bleed.

> "'Twere you my sins, my cruel sins,
> His chief tormentors were;
> Each of my grimes became a nail,
> And unbelief the spear."[10]

When a brother makes confession of his transgressions, when on his knees before God he humbles himself with many tears, I am sure the Lord thinks far more of the tears of repentance than he would do of the mere drops of human sympathy. "Weep for yourselves," says Christ, "rather than for me."

---

[10] Look on him who they pierced and mourn, Isaac Watts

When we look at the sufferings of Christ, we ought to sorrow deeply for the souls of all unregenerate men and women. Remember, dear friends, that what Christ suffered for us, these unregenerate ones must suffer for themselves, if they do not put their trust in Christ.

The woes which broke the Saviour's heart must crush theirs. Either Christ must die for me, or else I must die for myself the second death; if he did not carry the curse for me, then on me must it rest for ever and ever. Think, dear friends, there are some in this congregation who as yet have no interest in Jesu's blood, some sitting next to you, your nearest friends who, if they were now to close their eyes in death, would open them in hell! Think of that! Weep not for him, but for these. Perhaps they are your children, the objects of your fondest love, with no interest in Christ, without God and without hope in the world! Save your tears for them; Christ asks them not in sympathy for himself.

Think of the millions in this dark world! It is calculated that one soul passes from time into eternity every time the clock ticks! So numerous has the family of man now become, that there is a death every second; and when we know how very smell a proportion of the human race have even nominally received the cross — and there is none other name given under heaven among men whereby we must be saved.

Oh! What a black thought crosses our mind! What a collection of immortal souls dashes downwards to the pit every hour! Well might the Master say, "Weep not for me, but for yourselves."

You have, then, no true sympathy for Christ if you have not an earnest sympathy with those who would win souls for Christ. You may sit under a sermon, and feel a great deal, but your feeling is worthless unless it leads you to weep for yourselves and for your children.

How has it been with you? Have you repented of sin? Have you prayed for your fellow men? If not, may that picture of Christ fainting in the streets lead you to do so this morning.[11]

---

[11] The Procession of Sorrow – Sermon delivered March 1st 1863

5 – Christ's Fellow Sufferers

So they took Jesus, and he went out, bearing his own cross

(John 19:16 ESV)

There were two other cross-bearers in the throng; they were criminals; their crosses were just as heavy as the Lord's, and yet, at least, one of them had no sympathy with him, and his bearing the cross only led to his death, and not to his salvation.

I have sometimes met with people who have suffered much; they have lost money, they have worked hard all their lives, or they have laid for years upon a bed of sickness, and they therefore suppose that because they have suffered so much in this life, they shall thus escape the punishment of sin hereafter. I tell you, sirs, that criminal carried his cross and died on it; and you will carry your sorrows, and be damned with them, if you do not repent.

That impenitent thief went from the cross of his great agony — and it was agony indeed to die on a cross — he went to that place, to the flames of hell; and you, too, may go from the bed of sickness, and from the abode of poverty, to perdition, quite as readily as from the home of ease and the house of plenty. No sufferings of ours have anything to do with the atonement of sin. No blood but that which He has spilt, no groans but those which came from His heart, no suffering but that which was endured by Him, can ever make a recompense for sin.

Shake off the thought, any of you who suppose that God will have pity on you because you have endured affliction. You must consider Jesus, and not yourself; turn your eye to Christ, the great substitute for sinners, but never dream of trusting in yourselves.

Remember that when God saw Christ in the sinner's place he did not spare him, and when he finds you without Christ, he will not spare you. You have seen Jesus led away by his enemies; so shall you be dragged away by fiends to the place appointed for you. "Deliver him to the tormentors"[12] was the word of the king in the parable; it shall be fulfilled to you—"Depart from me you cursed ones everlasting fire, prepared for the devil and his angels."[13]

Jesus was deserted of God; and if he, who was only imputedly a sinner, was deserted, how much more shall you be? Oh! Sinner, if God hides his face from Christ, how much less will he spare you! He did not spare his Son the stripes. Did I not describe last Sabbath the knotted scourges which fell upon the Saviours back? What whips of steel for you, what knots of burning wire for you, when conscience shall smite you, when the law shall scourge you with its whip! Oh! Who would stand in your place, you richest, you merriest, you most self-righteous sinners — who would stand in your place?

---

[12] Matthew 18:34
[13] Matthew 25:41

I cannot roll up into one word all the mass of sorrows which met upon the head of Christ who died for us, therefore it is impossible for me to tell you what streams, what oceans of grief must roll over your spirit if you die as you now are. The scythe of death will cut some of you down before my voice shall warn you again!

Oh! Souls, I beseech you, by the agonies of Christ, by his wounds and by his blood, do not bring upon yourselves the curse; do not bear in your own person the awful wrath to come! May God deliver you! Trust in the Son of God and you shall never die.[14]

---

[14] The Procession of Sorrow – Sermon delivered March 1st 1863

6 – Yielding His Life

And when they came to the place that is called The Skull, there they crucified him, and the criminals, one on his right and one on his left. And Jesus said, "Father, forgive them, for they know not what they do." And they cast lots to divide his garments. And the people stood by, watching, but the rulers scoffed at him, saying, "He saved others; let him save himself, if he is the Christ of God, his Chosen One!" The soldiers also mocked him, coming up and offering him sour wine and saying, "If you are the King of the Jews, save yourself!" There was also an inscription over him, "This is the King of the Jews."

One of the criminals who were hanged railed at him, saying, "Are you not the Christ? Save yourself and us!" But the other rebuked him, saying, "Do you not fear God, since you are under the same sentence of condemnation? And we indeed

*justly, for we are receiving the due reward
of our deeds; but this man has done nothing
wrong." And he said, "Jesus, remember
me when you come into your
kingdom." And he said to him, "Truly, I say
to you, today you will be with me
in paradise."*

*It was now about the sixth hour, and there
was darkness over the whole land until the
ninth hour, while the sun's light failed.
And the curtain of the temple was torn in
two. Then Jesus, calling out with a loud
voice, said, "Father, into your hands
I commit my spirit!" And having said this he
breathed his last.*

(Luke 23:33-36 ESV)

They gave Jesus the place of dishonour. Reckoning him to be the worst criminal of the three, they put him between the other two. They heaped upon him the utmost scorn which they could give to a villain; and in so doing they unconsciously honoured him. Jesus always deserves the chief place wherever he is. In all things he must have the pre-eminence. He is King of sufferers as well as King of saints.

How startled they must have been to hear such words of forgiveness from one who was about to be put to death for a supposed crime! The men that drove the nails, the men that lifted up the tree, must have stared back with amazement when they heard Jesus talk to God as his Father, and pray for them: "Father, forgive them; for they know not what they do." Did ever Roman legionary hear such words before? No. They were so distinctly and diametrically opposed to the whole spirit of Rome. Theirs was blow for blow; only in the case of Jesus they gave blows where none had been received. The crushing cruelty of the Roman must have been startled indeed at such words as these, "Father, forgive them; for they know not what they do."

The gambling soldiers would not have dreamed that they were fulfilling Scriptures while they were gambling for the garments of the illustrious Sufferer on the cross; yet so it was. In the twenty-second Psalm, which so fully sets forth our Saviour's sufferings, and which he probably repeated while he hung on the tree, David wrote, "They divided my garments among them, and cast lots upon my clothing"[15]

And the people stood beholding, gazing, looking on the cruel spectacle. You and I would not have done that; there is a public sentiment which has trained us to hate the sight of cruelty, especially of deadly cruelty to one of our own race; but these people thought that they did no harm when they "stood beholding." They also were fulfilling the Scriptures; for the seventeenth verse of the twenty-second Psalm says, "They look and stare upon me"[16]

They laughed at him and made him the object of coarse jests. I imagine the scorn that they threw into their taunt: "If you be the king of the Jews;" that was a bit of their own. "Save yourself;" that they borrowed from the rulers. Sometimes a scoffer or a mocker cannot exhibit all the bitterness that is in his heart except by using borrowed terms, as these soldiers did.

---

[15] Psalm 22:18
[16] Psalm 22:17

John tells us that Pilate wrote this title, "King of the Jews", and that the chief priests tried in vain to get him to alter it. It was written in the three current languages of the time, so that the Greek, the Roman, and the Jew might alike understand who he was who was thus put to death.

He yielded his life. He did not die, as we have to do, because our appointed time has come, but willingly the great Sacrifice parted with his life: "He gave up the ghost." He was a willing sacrifice for guilty men.[17]

---

[17] Spurgeon's notes on Luke 23:33-46

7 – The Cries

It was most fitting that every word of our Lord upon the cross should be gathered up and preserved. As not a bone of him shall be broken, so not a word shall be lost. The Holy Spirit took special care that each of the sacred utterances should be fittingly recorded.

As these seven sayings were so faithfully recorded, it is not surprising that they have frequently been the subject of devout meditation. Fathers and confessors, preachers and divines have delighted to dwell upon every syllable of these matchless cries. These solemn sentences have shone like the seven golden candlesticks or the seven stars of the Apocalypse, and have lighted multitudes of men to him who spoke them. I cannot give you more than a mere taste of this rich subject, but I have been most struck with two ways of regarding our Lord's last words.

First, they teach and confirm many of the doctrines of our holy faith. *"Father, forgive them; for they know not what they do"*[18] is the first. Here is the forgiveness of sin—free forgiveness in answer to the Saviour's plea.

"Today you shall be with me in paradise"[19] Here is the safety of the believer in the hour of his departure, and his instant admission into the presence of his Lord. It is a blow at the fable of purgatory which strikes it to the heart.

"Woman, behold your son!"[20] This very plainly sets forth the true and proper humanity of Christ, who to the end recognised his human relationship to Mary, of whom he was born. Yet his language teaches us not to worship *her,* for he calls her "woman," but to honour him in whom his direst agony thought of her needs and griefs, as he also thinks of all his people, for these are his mother and sister and brother.

"Eloi, Eloi, lama sabachthani?"[21] This is the fourth cry, and it illustrates the penalty endured by our Substitute when he bore our

---

[18] Luke 23:34
[19] Luke 23:43
[20] John 19:26
[21] Matthew 27:46

sins, and so was forsaken of his God. The sharpness of that sentence is as keen as the very edge and point of the sword which pierced his heart.

"I thirst"[22] is the fifth cry, and its utterance teaches us the truth of Scripture, for all things were accomplished, that the Scripture might be fulfilled, and therefore our Lord said, "I thirst." Holy Scripture remains the basis of our faith, established by every word and act of our Redeemer.

The last word but one, *"It is finished"*[23] There is the complete justification of the believer, since the work by which he is accepted is fully accomplished.

The last of his last words is also taken from the Scriptures, and shows where his mind was feeding. He cried, *"Father, into your hands I commend my spirit."*[24] In that cry there is reconciliation to God. He who stood in our stead has finished all his work, and now his spirit comes back to the Father, and he brings us with him. Every word, therefore,

---

[22] John 19:28
[23] John 19:30
[24] Luke 23:46

you see teaches us some grand fundamental doctrine of our blessed faith.

A second mode of treating these seven cries is to view them as setting forth the person and offices of our Lord who uttered them.

"Father, forgive them; for they know not what they do" — here we see the Mediator interceding: Jesus standing before the Father pleading for the guilty.

"Truly I say to you, today you shall be with me in paradise" — this is the Lord Jesus in kingly power, opening with the key of David a door which none can shut, admitting into the gates of heaven the poor soul who had confessed him on the tree. Hail, everlasting King in heaven, you admit to your paradise whoever you will!

Then came, *"Woman, behold your son!"* where we see the Son of man in the gentleness of a son caring for his bereaved mother. In the former cry, as he opened Paradise, you saw the Son of God; now you see him who was truly born of a women, made under the law; and under the law you see him still, for he honours his mother and cares for her in the last article of death.

Then comes the *"My God, my God, why have you forsaken me?"* Here we behold his human soul in anguish, his inmost heart overwhelmed by the withdrawing of Jehovah's face, and made to cry out as if in perplexity and amazement.

"I thirst," is his human *body* tormented by grievous pain. Here you see how the mortal flesh had to share in the agony of the inward spirit.

"It is finished" is the last word but one, and there you see the perfected Saviour, the Captain of our salvation, who has completed the undertaking upon which he had entered, finished transgression, made an end of sin, and brought in everlasting righteousness.

The last expiring word in which he *commended his spirit to his Father,* is the note of acceptance for himself and for us all. As he commends his spirit into the Father's hand, so does he bring all believers close to God, and henceforth we are in the hand of the Father, who is greater than all, and none shall pluck us from there. Is not this a fertile field of thought?

Like the steps of a ladder or the links of a golden chain, there is a mutual dependence and interlinking of each of the cries, so that one leads to another and that to a third. Separately or in connection our Master's words overflow with instruction to thoughtful minds. [25]

---

[25] The Shortest of the Seven Cries – Sermon delivered April 14th, 1878

8 – The Plea for Ignorant Sinners

And Jesus said, Father, forgive them; for they know not what they do.

(Luke 23:34 ESV)

WHAT tenderness we have here; what self-forgetfulness; what almighty love! Jesus did not say to those who crucified him, "Begone!" One such word, and they must have all fled. When they came to take him in the garden, they went backward, and fell to the ground, when he spoke but a short sentence; and now that he is on the cross, a single syllable would have made the whole company fall to the ground, or flee away in fright.

Jesus says not a word in his own defence. When he prayed to his Father, he might justly have said, "Father, note what they do to your beloved Son. Judge them for the wrong they do to him who loves them, and who has done all he can for them." But there is no prayer against them in the words that Jesus utters. It was written of old, by the prophet Isaiah, "He made intercession for the transgressors"[26] and here it is fulfilled. He pleads for his murderers, "Father, forgive them."

He does not say, "Why do you this? Why pierce the hands that fed you? Why nail the feet that followed after you in mercy? Why mock the Man who loved to bless you?" No, not a word even of gentle rebuke, much less anything like a curse. "Father, forgive them." Jesus take the place of a pleader, a pleader for those who were committing murder upon himself. Blessed be his name!

We who have been forgiven, we who have been washed in the blood of the Lamb, we once sinned, in a great measure, through ignorance. Jesus says, "They know not what they do." Now, I shall appeal to you, brothers and sisters, when you lived under the dominion of Satan, and served yourselves

---

[26] Isaiah 53:12

and sin, was there not a measure of ignorance in it?

It is true, first, that we were ignorant of *the awful meaning of sin.* We began to sin as children; we knew that it was wrong, but we did not know all that sin meant. We went on to sin as young men; we plunged into much wickedness. We knew it was wrong; but we did not see the end from the beginning. It did not appear to us as rebellion against God. We did not think that we were presumptuously defying God, setting at naught his wisdom, defying his power, deriding his love, spurning his holiness; yet we were doing that. There is an abysmal depth in sin. You cannot see the bottom of it. When we rolled sin under our tongue as a sweet morsel, we did not know all the terrible ingredients compounded in that deadly bittersweet.

We did not know, at that time, *God's great love to us.* I did not know that he had chosen me from before the foundation of the world; I never dreamed of that. I did not know that Christ stood for me as my substitute, to redeem me from among men. I did not know the love of Christ, did not understand it then.

You did not know that you were sinning against eternal love, against infinite compassion, against a distinguishing love such as God had fixed on you from eternity. So far, we knew not what we did.

We did not know that, in that rejection, we were crucifying him. We were denying his Godhead, or else we should have worshipped him. We were denying his love, or else we should have yielded to him. We were practically, in every act of sin, taking the hammer and the nails, and fastening Christ to the cross, but we did not know it. Perhaps, if we had known it, we should not have crucified the Lord of glory. We did know we were doing wrong; but we did not know all the wrong that we were doing.

We used to think, some of us, that we had a righteousness of our own. We had been to church regularly. We were christened; we were confirmed; or, we rejoiced that we never had either of those things done to us. Thus, we put our confidence in ceremonies, or the absence of ceremonies. We said our prayers; we read a chapter in the bible night and morning. But there we rested; we were righteous in our own esteem. We had not any particular sin to confess, nor any reason to lie in the dust before the throne of God's majesty. We were about as good as we could be; and we did not know that we were even then perpetrating the highest insult upon Christ; for, if we were not sinners, why did Christ die; and, if we had a righteousness of our own which was good enough, why did Christ come here to work out a righteousness for us?

We thought we were pleasing God by our religiousness, by our outward performances, by our ecclesiastical correctness; but all the while we were setting up anti-Christ in the place of Christ. We were making out that Christ was not wanted; we were robbing him of his office and glory! Alas! Christ would say of us, with regard to all these things, "They know not what they do." I want you to look quietly at the time past when you served sin, and see whether there was not a darkness upon your mind, a blindness in your spirit, so that you did not know what you did.[27]

---

[27] Christ's Plea for Ignorant Sinners – Sermon Delivered July 3rd, 1892

9 – No Excuse

And Jesus said, Father, forgive them; for they know not what they do.

(Luke 23:34 ESV)

God gives us the law, and we are bound to keep it. If I erred through not knowing the law, it was still a sin. Under the Mosaic law, there were sins of ignorance, and for these there were special offerings. The ignorance did not blot out the sin.

Many of us, who are now Christ's people, would have known much more about our Lord if we had given him more careful consideration in our earlier days. A man will think about taking a wife, he will think about making a business, he will think about buying a horse or a cow; but he will not think about the claims of Christ, and the claims of the Most High God; and this renders his ignorance wilful, and inexcusable.

There were times when you knew that such an action was wrong. You looked at the gain it would bring you, and you sold your soul for that price, and deliberately did what you were well aware was wrong. Are there not some here, saved by Christ, who must confess that, at times, they did violence to their conscience? They drove the Spirit away from them, distinctly knowing what they were doing. Let us bow before God in the silence of our hearts, and own to all of this. We hear the Master say, "Father, forgive them; for they know not what they do." Let us add our own tears as we say, "And forgive us, also, because in some things we did know; in all things we might have known; but we were ignorant for lack of thought.

When a man is ignorant, and does not know what he ought to do, what should he do? Well, he should do nothing till he does know. But here is the mischief of it, that *when we did not know, yet we chose to do the wrong thing.* If we did not know, why did we not choose the right thing? But, being in the dark, we never turned to the right; but always blundered to the left from sin to sin. Does not this show us how depraved our hearts are? Though we are seeking to be right, when we were let alone, we go wrong of ourselves. Leave a child alone; leave a man alone; leave a tribe alone without teaching and instruction; what comes of it? Why, the same as when you leave a field alone. It never, by any chance, produces wheat or barley. Leave it alone, and there are rank weeds, and thorns, and briars, showing that the natural set of the soil is towards producing that which is worthless.

O friends, confess the evil of your hearts as well as the evil of your lives, in that, when you did not know, yet, having a perverse instinct, you chose the evil, and refuse the good; and, when you did not know enough of Christ, and did not think enough of him to know whether you ought to have him or not, you would not have come unto him that you might have life.

You needed light; but you shut your eyes to the sun. You were thirsty; but you would not drink of the living spring; and so your ignorance, though it was there, was a criminal ignorance, which you must confess before the Lord. Oh, come you to the cross, you who have been there before, and have lost your burden there! Come and confess your guilt over again; and clasp that cross afresh, and look to him who bled upon it, and praise his dear name that he once prayed for you, "Father forgive them; for they know not what they do."[28]

---

[28] Christ's Plea for Ignorant Sinners – Sermon Delivered July 3rd, 1892

10 - Our Lord Pleads For Us

And Jesus said, Father, forgive them; for they know not what they do.

(Luke 23:34 ESV)

Did you notice when it was that Jesus pleaded? It was, *while they were crucifying him.*

They had not just driven in the nails, they had lifted up the cross, and dished it down into its socket, and dislocated all his bones, so that he could say, "I am poured out like water, and all my bones are out of joint." Ah, dear friends, it was then that instead of a cry or groan, this dear Son of God said, "Father, forgive them; for they know not what they do." They did not ask for forgiveness for themselves, Jesus asked for forgiveness for them. Their hands were imbrued in his blood; and it was then, even then, that he prayed for them. Let us think of the great love with which he loved us, even while we were yet sinners, when we rioted in sin, when we drank it down as the ox drinks down water. Even then he prayed for us.

"While we were yet without strength, in due time Christ died for the ungodly"[29] Bless his name! He prayed for you when you did not pray for yourself. He prayed for you when you were crucifying him.

Think of his plea, *he pleads his Sonship.* He says, "*Father,* forgive them." He was the Son of God, and he put his divine Sonship into the scale on our behalf. He seems to say, "Father, as I am your Son, grant me this request, and pardon these rebels. Father, forgive them."

The rights of Christ were very great. He was the Son of the Highest. "Light of light, very God of very God"[30], the second Person in the Divine Trinity; and he puts that Sonship here before God and says, "Father, Father, forgive them." Oh, the power of that word from the Son's lip when he is wounded, when he is in agony, when he is dying! He says, "Father,

---

[29] Romans 5:6
[30] Nicene Creed

Father, grant my one request; O Father, forgive them; for they know not what they do;" and the great Father bows his head, to signify that the petition is granted.

Then notice, that Jesus here, silently, *pleads his sufferings.* The attitude of Christ when he prayed this prayer is very noteworthy. His hands were stretched upon the transverse beam; his feet were fastened to the upright tree; and there he pleaded. Silently his hands and feet were pleading, and his agonized body from the very sinew and muscle pleaded with God. His sacrifice was presented complete; and so it is his cross that takes up the plea, "Father, forgive them." O blessed Christ! It is thus that we have been forgiven, for his Sonship and his cross have pleaded with God, and have prevailed on our behalf.

I love this prayer, also, because of the *indistinctness* of it. It is "Father, forgive them." He does not say, "Father, forgive the soldiers who have nailed me here." He includes them. Neither does he say, "Father, forgive sinners in ages to come who will sin against me." But he means them. Jesus does not mention them by any accusing name:

"Father, forgive my enemies. Father, forgive my murderers." No, there is no word of accusation upon those dear lips. "Father, forgive them." Now into that pronoun "them" I feel that I can crawl Can you get in there? Oh, by a humble faith, appropriate the cross of Christ by trusting in it; and get into that big little word "them"! It seems like a chariot of mercy that has come down to earth into which a man may step, and it shall bear him up to heaven. "Father, forgive them."

Notice, also, what it was that Jesus asked for; to omit that, would be to leave out the very essence of his prayer. *He asked for full absolution for his enemies:* "Father, forgive them. Do not punish them; forgive them. Do not remember their sin; forgive it, blot it out; throw it into the depths of the sea. Remember it not, my Father. Mention it not against them any more for ever. Father, forgive them."

Oh, blessed prayer, for the forgiveness of God is broad and deep! When man forgives, he leaves the remembrance of the wrong behind; but when God pardons, he says, "I will forgive their iniquity, and I will remember their sin no more." It is this that Christ asked for you and me long before we had any repentance, or any faith; and in answer to that prayer, we were brought to feel our sin, we were brought to confess it, and to believe in him; and now, glory be to his name, we can bless him for having pleaded for us, and obtained the forgiveness of all our sins.[31]

---

[31] Christ's Plea for Ignorant Sinners – Sermon Delivered July 3rd, 1892

11 – Rejoice in the Pardon

And Jesus said, Father, forgive them; for they know not what they do.

(Luke 23:34 ESV)

I have a letter, in my pocket, from a man of education and standing, who has been an agnostic; he says that he was a sarcastic agnostic, and he writes praising God, and invoking every blessing upon my head for bringing him to the Saviour's feet. He says, "I was without happiness for this life, and without hope for the next."

I believe that that is a truthful description of many an unbeliever. What hope is there for the world to come apart from the cross of Christ? The best hope such a man has is that he may die the death of a dog, and there may be an end of him. I feel so sorry for many of the devout and earnest friends, for I do not know what their hope is. They do not hope to go to heaven yet, at any rate; some purgatorial pains must be endured first. Ah, this is a poor, poor faith to die on, to have such a hope as that to trouble your last thoughts.

I do not know of any religion but that of Christ Jesus which tells us of sin pardoned, absolutely pardoned. Now, listen. Our teaching is not that, when you come to die, you may, perhaps, find out that it is all right, but, "Beloved, now we are the sons of God." "He that believes in the Son has everlasting life." He has it now, and he knows it, and he rejoices in it. We rejoice in the pardon Christ has obtained for us. We are pardoned. I hope that the larger portion of this audience can say, "By the grace of God, we know that we are washed in the blood of the Lamb."

Pardon has come to us through Christ's plea. Our hope lies in the plea of Christ, and specifically in his death. If Jesus paid my debt, and he did it if I am a believer in him, then I am out of debt. If Jesus bore the penalty of my sin, and he did it if I am a believer, then there is no penalty for me to pay, for we can say to him,

"Complete atonement you have made,
And to the utmost farthing paid
Whate'er your people owed:
Nor can his wrath on me take place,
If shelter'd in your righteousness,
And sprinkled with your blood.

"If you have my discharge procured,
And freely in my room endured
The whole of wrath divine:
Payment God cannot twice demand,
First of my bleeding Surety's hand,
And then again at mine."[32]

If Christ has borne my punishment, I shall never bear it. Oh, what joy there is in this blessed assurance! Your hope that you are pardoned lies in this, that Jesus died. Those dear wounds of his bled for you.

If you rejoice that you are pardoned, *show your gratitude by your imitation of Christ.* There was never before such a plea as this, "Father, forgive them; for they know not what they do." Plead like that for others.

---

[32] From whence this fear and unbelief, Augustus Toplady

Has anybody been injuring you? Are there persons who slander you? Pray to-night, "Father, forgive them; for they know not what they do." Let us always render good for evil, blessing for cursing; and when we are called to suffer through the wrong-doing of others, let us believe that they would not act as they do if it were not because of their ignorance. Let us pray for them; and make their very ignorance the plea for their forgiveness: "Father, forgive them; for they know not what they do."

Brethren, I see *reason for hope in the very ignorance that surrounds us.* I see hope for this poor city of ours, hope for this poor country, hope for Africa, China, and India. "They know not what they do." Here is a strong argument in their favour, for they are more ignorant than we were. They know less of the evil of sin, and less of the hope of eternal life, than we do. Send up this petition, you people of God! Heap your prayers together with cumulative power, send up this fiery shaft of prayer, straight to the heart of God, while Jesus from his throne shall add his prevalent intercession, "Father, forgive them; for they know not what they do."

If there be any unconverted people here, and I know that there are some, we will mention them in our private devotion, as well as in the public assembly; and we will pray for them in words like these, "Father, forgive them; for they know not what they do." May God bless you all, for Jesus Christ's sake! [33]

---

[33] Christ's Plea for Ignorant Sinners – Sermon Delivered July 3rd, 1892

12 – Perserverance in Prayer

And Jesus said, Father, forgive them; for they know not what they do.

(Luke 23:34 ESV)

Our Lord was at this moment enduring the first pains of crucifixion; the executioners had just driven the nails through his hands and feet. He was brought into a condition of extreme weakness by the agony of the night in Gethsemane, and by the scourging and cruel mocking which he had endured all through the morning, from Caiaphas, Pilate, Herod, and the Praetorian guards. Yet neither the weakness of the past, nor the pain of the present, could prevent him from continuing in prayer.

The Lamb of God was silent to men, but he was not silent to God. He had not a word to say in his own defence to man, but he continues in his heart crying unto his Father, and no pain and no weakness can silence his holy supplications. What an example our Lord presents to us! Let us continue in prayer so long as our heart beats; let no suffering drive us away from the throne of grace, but rather let it drive us closer to it.

Our blessed Redeemer persevered in prayer even when the cruel iron tore his tender nerves, and blow after blow of the hammer jarred his whole frame with anguish; and this perseverance may be accounted for by the fact that he was so in the habit of prayer that he could not cease from it. Those long nights upon the cold mountain side, those many days which had been spent in solitude had formed in him a habit so powerful, that the severest torments could not stay its force.

Yet it was more than habit. Our Lord was baptised in the spirit of prayer; he lived in it, it lived in him, it had come to be an element of his nature. The extreme trial to which he now submitted himself could not prevent his holding fast his Sonship. His prayer begins, "Father." It was not without meaning that he taught us when we pray to say, "Our Father," for our prevalence in prayer will much depend upon our confidence in our relationship to God. Under great losses and crosses, one is adapt to think that God is not dealing with us as a father with a child, but rather as a severe judge with a condemned criminal; but the cry of Christ, when he is brought to an extremity which we shall never reach, betrays no faltering in the spirit of sonship.

In Gethsemane, when the bloody sweat fell fast upon the ground, his bitterest cry commenced with, *"My Father,"* asking that if it were possible the cup of gall might pass from him; he pleaded with the Lord as his Father, even as he over and over again had called him on that dark and doleful night. Here, again, in this, the first of his seven expiring cries, it is "Father." O that the Spirit that makes us cry, "Abba, Father," may never cease his operations!

More remarkable, however, is the fact that our Lord's prayer to his Father was not for himself. It is, "Father, forgive *them."* The cry is altogether unselfish. What a soul of compassion was in the Crucified! How Godlike, how divine! Was there ever such a one before him, who, even in the very pangs of death, offers as his first prayer an intercession for others? Let this unselfish spirit be in you also. Love your neighbours as yourselves, and as Christ has set before you this paragon of unselfishness, seek to follow him, treading in his steps.

There is, however, a crowning jewel in this diadem of glorious love. The prayer was not alone for others, but it was for his cruellest enemies. His enemies who were there and then murdering him. Not in cold blood did the Saviour pray, after he had forgotten the injury, and could the more easily forgive it, but while the first red drops of blood were spurting on the hands which drove the nails; while the hammer was stained with crimson gore, his blessed mouth poured out the fresh warm prayer, "Father, forgive them, for they know not what they do."

How sublime is this prayer if viewed in such a light! It stands alone upon a mount of solitary glory. I feel as though I would rather kneel before my Lord's cross at this moment than stand in this pulpit to talk to you. I want to adore him; I worship him in heart for that prayer; if I knew nothing else of him but this one prayer, I must adore him, for that one matchless plea for mercy convinces me most overwhelmingly of the deity of him who offered it, and fills my heart with reverent affection.[34]

---

[34] The First Cry from the Cross – Sermon delivered October 24th, 1869

13 – Gracious Intercession

And Jesus said, Father, forgive them; for they know not what they do.

(Luke 23:34 ESV)

Our Lord's intercession is *most gracious.* Those for whom our Lord prayed, according to the text, did not deserve his prayer. They had done nothing which could call forth from him a reward for their endeavours in his service; on the contrary, they were most undeserving persons, who had conspired to put him to death.

They had crucified him, taking away his innocent life. They certainly never asked him to pray for them — it was the last thought in their minds to say, "Intercede for us, you dying King! Offer petitions on our behalf, you Son of God!" I will venture to believe the prayer itself, when they heard it, was either disregarded, and passed over with contemptuous indifference, or perhaps it was caught as a theme for jest.

Our Saviour prayed for persons who did not deserve the prayer, but, on the contrary, merited a curse — persons who did not ask for the prayer, and even scoffed at it when they heard it. Even so in heaven there stands the great High Priest, who pleads for guilty men. There are none on earth that deserve his intercession. He pleads for none on the supposition that they do deserve it. He stands there to plead as the just One on the behalf of the unjust. Remember, if there be nothing good in you, and if there be everything conceivable that is malignant and bad, none of these things can be any barrier to prevent Christ's exercising the office of Intercessor for you. Even for you he will plead. Come, put your case into his hands.

A second quality of his intercession is its *careful spirit.* You notice in the prayer, "Father, forgive them, for they know not what they do." Our Saviour did, as it were, look his enemies through to find something in them that he could urge in their favour; but he could not see nothing until his wisely affectionate eye lit upon their ignorance: "they know not what they do." Christ is no careless advocate for his people. He knows your precise condition at this moment, and the exact state of your heart with regard to the temptation through which you are passing; more than that, he foresees the temptation which is awaiting you, and in his intercession he takes note of the future event which his eye beholds. "Satan hath desired to have you, that he may sift you like wheat; but I have prayed for you that your faith fail not."[35]

He knows us better than we know ourselves. He understands every secret grief and groaning. You need not trouble yourself about the wording of your prayer, he will put the wording right.

It is interesting to note, that the intercession continues. If our Saviour might have paused from intercessory prayer, it was surely when they fastened him to the tree; when they were guilty of direct acts of deadly violence to his divine person, he might then have

---

[35] Luke 22:31

ceased to present petitions on their behalf. But sin cannot tie the tongue of our interceding Friend! Oh, what comfort is here! You have sinned, believer, you have grieved his Spirit, but you have not stopped that potent tongue which pleads for you. You have been unfruitful, perhaps, my brother, and like the barren tree, you deserve to be cut down; but your lack of fruitfulness has not withdrawn the Intercessor from his place.

He lives, and while he lives he pleads; and while there is a sinner upon earth to be saved, there shall be an intercessor in heaven to plead for him. These are but fragments of thought, but they will help you, I hope, to realise the intercession of your great High Priest.

The intercession prevailed. Many of those for whom he prayed were forgiven. Do you remember that day when Peter stood up with the eleven, and charged the people with wicked hands they had crucified and slain the Saviour, three thousand became believers in him, and were baptised in his name. That was an answer to Jesus' prayer.

The priest were at the bottom of the Lord's murder, they were the most guilty; but it is said, "a great company also of the priests believed."[36]

He never pleads in vain. With bleeding hands, he won the day; with feet fastened to the wood, he was victorious; forsaken of God and despised of the people, he was triumphant in his pleas; how much more so now the tiara is about his brow, his hand grasp the universal sceptre, and his feet are shod with silver sandals, and he is crowned King of kings, and Lord of lords!

O you trembling believers, trust him with your concerns! [37]

---

[36] Acts6:7

[37] The First Cry from the Cross – Sermon delivered October 24th, 1869

14 – The Work of the Church

And Jesus said, Father, forgive them; for they know not what they do.

(Luke 23:34 ESV)

As Christ was, so his church is to be in this world. Christ came into this world not to be ministered unto, but to minister, not to be honoured, but to save others. His church, when she understands her work, will perceive that she is not here to gather to herself wealth or honour; she is here to live unselfishly, and if need be, to die for the deliverance of the lost sheep.

The prayer on the cross was an unselfish one. He does not remember himself in it. Such ought to be the church's prayer, the church's active intercession on the behalf of sinners. She ought to live never for herself, but ever for the lost sons of men.

These places are not built that you may sit here comfortably, and hear something that shall make you pass away your Sundays with pleasure. A church which does not exist to do good in the slums, and dens of the city, is a church that has no reason to justify its longer existing.

A church that does not exist to fight with evil, to destroy error, to put down falsehood; a church that does not exist to take the side of the poor, to denounce injustice and to hold up righteousness, is a church that has no right to be. Not for yourself, O church, do you exist, any more than Christ existed for himself. His glory was that he laid aside his glory, and the glory of the church is when she lays aside her respectability and her dignity, and counts it to be her glory to gather together the outcast. To rescue souls from hell and lead to God, to hope, to heaven, this is her heavenly occupation. O that the church would always feel this!

Nothing is sought for these people except that which concerns their souls, Father, *forgive* them." And I believe the church will do well when she recollects that she wrestles not with flesh and blood, nor with principalities and powers, but with spiritual wickedness. I believe that the more the church of God strains after, before God, the forgiveness of sinners, and the more she seeks prayer to teach sinners what sin is, and what the blood of Christ is, and what the hell that must follow if sin be not washed out, and what the heaven is which will be ensured to all those who are cleansed from sin, the better.

O let nothing turn you aside from your divine errand of mercy to undying souls. This is your one business. Tell to sinners that sin will damn them, that Christ alone can take away sin, and make this the one passion of your souls, "Father, forgive them, forgive them! Let them know how to be forgiven. Let them be actually forgiven, and let me never rest except as I am the means of bringing sinners to be forgiven, even the guiltiest of them."

Christ prayed for the wicked, the most wicked of the wicked, that crew that had surrounded his cross! He prayed for his persecutors; the very persons who were most at enmity with him, lay nearest to his heart. Church of God, your mission is not to the respectable few who will gather about your ministers to listen respectfully to their words; your mission is not to the elite, the intelligent who will criticise your words and pass judgment upon every syllable of your teaching; your mission is not to those who treat you kindly, generously, affectionately. Though these will be among you; your great errand is to the harlot, to the thief, to the swearer and the drunkard, to the most depraved and debauched. If no one else cares for these, the church must, and they should be first in her prayers.

The gospel is also meant for those who persecute religion; it aims its arrows of love against the hearts of his foes. If there be any whom we should first seek to bring to Jesus, it should be those who are the farthest off and the most opposed to the gospel of Christ.

Have we not around us hundreds of thousands to whom the simplest truths of the gospel would be the greatest novelties? What hope we have when we read the Saviour's prayer — it helps us to hope while we cry, "Forgive them, for they know not what they do."[38]

---

[38] The First Cry from the Cross – Sermon delivered October 24th, 1869

15 – Look at Him

He trusts in God; let God deliver him now, if he desires him. For he said, 'I am the Son of God.'

(Matthew 27:43 ESV)

These words are a fulfilment of the prophecy contained in the Psalms.

"All they that see me laugh me to scorn: they shoot out the lip, they shake the head, saying, He trusted on the Lord that he would deliver him: let him deliver him, seeing he delighted in him."[39]

Our Lord answers the ancient prophecy to the letter.

It is very painful to the heart to picture our blessed Master in his death-agonies, surrounded by a wild multitude, who watched him and mocked him, made sport of his prayer and insulted his faith. Nothing was sacred to them: they invaded the Holy of holies of his confidence in God, and

---

[39] Psalm 23:7

taunted him concerning that faith in Jehovah which they were compelled to admit.

See, dear friends, what an evil thing is sin, since the Sin-bearer suffers so bitterly to make atonement for it! See, also, the shame of sin, since even the Prince of Glory, when bearing the consequences of it, is covered with contempt! Behold, also, how he loved us! For our sake he "endured the cross, despising the shame"[40]. He loved us so much that even scorn of the cruellest sort he deigned to bear, that he might take away our shame and enable us to look up unto God.

Beloved, the treatment of our Lord Jesus Christ by men is the clearest proof of total depravity which can possibly be required or discovered. Those must be stony hearts indeed which can laugh at a dying Saviour, and mock even at his faith in God! Compassion would seem to have deserted humanity, while malice sat supreme on the throne. Painful as the picture is, it will do you good to paint it. You will need neither canvas, nor brush, nor palette, nor colours. Let your thoughts draw the outline, and your

---

[40] Hebrews 12:2

love fill in the detail; I shall not complain if imagination heightens the colouring. The Son of God, whom angels adore with veiled faces, is pointed at with scornful fingers by men who thrust out the tongue and mockingly exclaim, "He trusted on the Lord that he would deliver him: let him deliver him, seeing he delighted in him."

While we see our Lord here in his sorrow and his shame as our substitute, we must not forget that he also is there as our representative. That which appears in many a psalm to relate to David is found in the Gospels to refer to Jesus, our Lord. Often, the student of the Psalm will say to himself, "Of whom does the prophet speak?" He will have to disentangle the threads sometimes, and mark off that which belongs to David and that which relates to the Son of God; and frequently he will not be able to disentangle the threads at all, because they are one, and may relate both to David, and to David's Lord.

This is meant to show us that the life of Christ is an epitome of the life of his people. He not only suffers for us as our substitute, but he suffers before us as our pattern. In him we see what we have in our measure to endure. "As he is, so are we also in this world".[41] We also must be crucified to the world, and we may look for somewhat of those tests of faith and taunts of derision which go with such a crucifixion.

"Marvel not if the world hate you" [42]

You, too, must suffer without the gate. Not for the world's redemption, but for the accomplishment of divine purposes in you, and through you to the sons of men, you must be made to know the cross and its shame. Christ is the mirror of the church. What the head endured every member of the body will also have to endure in its measure. Let us read the text in this light, and come to it saying to ourselves, "Here we see what Jesus suffered in our stead, and we learn to love him with all our souls. Here, too, we see, as in a prophecy, how great things we are to suffer for his sake at the hands of men." May the Holy Spirit help us in our meditation, so that we may more

---

[41] 1 John 4:17
[42] 1 John 3:13

ardently love our Lord, who suffered for us, and may carefully arm ourselves with the same mind which enabled him to endure such contradiction of sinners against himself.[43]

---

[43] Let Him Deliver Him Now – Sermon delivered June 17th, 1888

16 – He Trusted in God

He trusts in God; let God deliver him now, if he desires him. For he said, 'I am the Son of God.'

(Matthew 27:43 ESV)

Let me invite you to observe the acknowledgement which these mockers made of our Lord's faith: "He trusted in God."

The Saviour did not wear any peculiar garb or token by which he let men know that he trusted in God. He was not a recluse, neither did he join some little knot of separatists, who boasted their peculiar trust in Jehovah. Although our Saviour was separate from sinners, he was a man among men, and he went in and out among the multitude as one of themselves. His one peculiarity was that "he trusted in God." This peculiarity had been visible even to that ungodly multitude who least of all cared to perceive a spiritual point of character. Had these scorners ever mocked anyone before for such a matter as this? I think not. Your faith had been so manifest in our Lord's daily life that the crowd cried out aloud, "He trusted in God."

How did they know? I suppose they could not help seeing that *he made much of God* in his teaching, in his life, and in his miracles. Whenever Jesus spoke it was always godly talk; and if it was not always distinctly about God, it was always about things that related to God, that came from God, that led to God, that magnified God. A man may be fairly judged by that which he makes most of. The ruling passion is a fair gauge of the heart. What a soul-ruler faith is! It sways the man as the rudder guides the ship. When a man once gets to live by faith in God, it influences his thoughts, it masters his purposes, it flavours his words, it puts a tone into his actions, and it comes out in everything by ways and means most natural and unconstrained, till men perceive that they have to do with a man who makes much of God.

In addition to observing that Jesus made much of God, men came to note that he was *a trusting man, and not self-confident.* Certain persons are very proud because they are self-made men. I will do them the credit to admit that they heartily worship their maker. Self made them, and they worship self. We have among us individuals who are self-confident, and almost all-sufficient; they sneer at those who do not succeed, for *they* can succeed anywhere at anything. The world to them is a football which they can kick where they like. A vat of sufficiency ferments within their ribs! There was nothing of that sort of thing in our Lord.

Those who watched him did not say that he had great self-reliance and a noble spirit of self-confidence. No, no! They said, "He trusted in God." Indeed it was so. The words that he spoke he spoke not of himself, and the great deeds that he did he never boasted of, but said "the Father that dwells in me, he does the works"[44] He was a truster in God, not a boaster in self. Self-confidence is the death of confidence in God; reliance upon talent, tact, experience, and things of that kind, kills faith. Oh that we may know what

---

[44] John 14:10

faith means, and so look out of ourselves and quit the evil confidence which looks within!

It is evident that the Lord Jesus *trusted in God openly* since the crowd proclaimed it. Some good people try to exercise faith on the sly: they practise it in snug corners, and in lonely hours, but they are afraid to say much before others, for fear their faith should not see the promise fulfilled. They dare not say, with David, "My soul shall make her boast in the Lord: the humble shall hear thereof, and be glad".[45] This secrecy robs God of his honour. Why should we be ashamed? Let us throw down the gauge of battle to earth and hell. God, the true and faithful, deserves to be trusted without limit. Trust your all with him, and be not ashamed of having done so. Our Saviour was not ashamed of trusting in his God. Jesus lived by faith. If so glorious a person as the only begotten Son of God lived here by faith in God, how are you and I to live except by trust in God?

If nobody else trusts in God, let us do so; and thus may we uplift a testimony to the honour

---

[45] Psalm 34:2

of his faithfulness. When we die, may this be our epitaph—"He trusted in God."[46]

---

[46] Let Him Deliver Him Now – Sermon delivered June 17th, 1888

17 – The Benefits of Trust

He trusts in God; let God deliver him now, if he desires him. For he said, 'I am the Son of God.'

(Matthew 27:43 ESV)

Jesus' faith was personal: that the Father would deliver him. Blessed is that faith which can reach its arm of compassion around the world, but that faith must begin at home. Of what use is the longest arm if it is not fixed to the man himself at the shoulder? "He trusted in the Lord that he would deliver him." Come, beloved, have you such a faith in the living God? Do you trust in God through Christ Jesus that he will save you?

Yes, you poor, unworthy one, the Lord will deliver you if you trust him. Yes, poor woman, or unknown man, the Lord can help you in your present trouble, and in every other, and he will do so if you trust him to that end. May the Holy Spirit lead you to first trust the Lord Jesus for the pardon of sin, and then to trust in God for all things.

Let us pause a minute. Let a man trust in God; not in fiction but in fact, and he will find that he has solid rock under his feet. Let him trust about his own daily needs and trials, and rest assured that the Lord will actually appear for him, and he will not be disappointed. Such a trust in God is a very *reasonable* thing; its absence is most unreasonable.

If there be a God, he knows all about my case. If he made my ear he can hear me; if he made my eye he can see me; and therefore he perceives my condition. If he be my Father, as he says he is, he will certainly care for me, and will help me in my hour of need if he can. We are sure that he can, for he is omnipotent. Is there anything unreasonable, then, in trusting in God that he will deliver us?

I venture to say that if all the forces in the universe were put together, and all the kindly intents of all who are our friends were put together, and we were then to rely upon those united forces and intents, we should not have a thousandth part so much justification for our confidence as when we depend upon God, whose intents and forces are infinitely greater than those of all the world beside.

"It is better to trust in the Lord than to put confidence in man; it is better to trust in the Lord than to put confidence in princes"[47]

If you view things in the white light of pure reason, it is infinitely more reasonable to trust in the living God than in all his creatures put together.

It is also extremely *comfortable* to trust in God. To roll your burden upon the Lord, since he will sustain you, is a blessed way of being rid of care. We know him to be faithful, and as powerful as he is faithful; and our dependence upon him is the solid foundation of a profound peace.

While it is comfortable, it is also *uplifting.* If you trust in men, the best of men, you are likely to be lowered by your trust. We are apt to cringe before these who patronize us. If

---

[47] Psalm 118:8-9

your prosperity depends upon a person's smile, you are tempted to pay homage even when it is undeserved. The old saying mentions a certain person as "knowing on which side his bread is buttered." Thousands are practically degraded by their trusting in men. But when our reliance is upon the living God we are raised by it, and elevated both morally and spiritually. You may bow in deepest reverence before God, and yet there will be no fawning. You may lie in the dust before the Majesty of heaven, and yet not be dishonoured by your humility; in fact, it is our greatness to be nothing in the presence of the Most High.

This confidence in God makes men *strong.* I should advise the enemy not to oppose the man who trusts in God. In the long run he will be beaten, as Haman found it with Mordecai. He had been warned of this by Zeresh, his wife, and his wise men, who said, "If Mordecai be of the seed of the Jews, before whom you have begun to fall, you shalt not prevail against him, but shalt surely fall before him"[48] Contend not with a man who has God at his back.

When a believer stands out against evil he may be sure that the Lord of hosts will not be far away. The enemy shall hear the dash of his horse-hoof and the blast of his trumpet, and shall flee before him. Wherefore be of good courage, and compel the world to say of you, "He trusted in the Lord that he would deliver him."[49]

---

[48] Esther 6:13
[49] Let Him Deliver Him Now – Sermon delivered June 17th, 1888

18 – Hear the Taunt

He trusts in God; let God deliver him now, if he desires him. For he said, 'I am the Son of God.'

(Matthew 27:43 ESV)

This taunt against Jesus has *the appearance of being very logical*. If God has promised to deliver us, and we have openly professed to believe the promise, it is only natural that others should say, "Let us see whether he does deliver him. This man believes that the Lord will help him; and he must help him, or else the man's faith is a delusion." This is the sort of test to which we ourselves would have put others before our conversion, and we cannot object to be proved in the same manner ourselves.

It is peculiarly painful to have this stern inference driven home to you in the hour of sorrow. In the time of depression of spirit it is hard to have one's faith questioned, or the ground on which it stands made a matter of dispute. Either to be mistaken in one's belief, or to have no real faith, or to find the ground of one's faith fail is an exceedingly grievous thing. Yet as our Lord was not spared this painful ordeal, we must not expect to be kept clear of it, and Satan knows well how to work these questions, till the poison of them sets the blood on fire. He hurls this fiery dare into the soul, till the man is sorely wounded, and can scarcely hold his ground.

Much emphasis lies in its being *in the present tense:* "He trusted in God that he would deliver him: let him deliver him *now*". This is how Satan assails us, using our present and pressing tribulations as the barbs of his arrows.

A Christian man may be beaten in business, he may fail to meet all demands, and then Satan yells, "Let him deliver him *now.*" The poor man has been out of work for two or three months, tramping the streets of London until he has worn out his boots; he has been brought to his last penny. I think I hear the laugh of the Prince of Darkness as he cries, "Let him deliver him *now.*" Or else the believer is very ill in body, and low in spirit, and then Satan howls, "Let him deliver him *now.*" Some of us have been in very trying positions. We were moved with indignation because of deadly error, and we spoke plainly, but men refused to hear. Those we relied upon deserted us; good men sought their own ease and would not march with us, and we had to bear testimony for despised truth alone, until we were ourselves despised. Then the adversary shouted, "Let him deliver him *now.*" Be it so! We do not refuse the test. Our God whom we serve will deliver us. We will not bow down to modern thought nor worship the image which human wisdom has set up. Our God is God both of hills and of valleys. He will not fail his servants, albeit that for a while he forbears that he may try their faith. We dare accept the test, and say, "Let him deliver us *now.*"

Yes, the test will come again and again. May the taunts of adversaries only make us ready for the sterner ordeals of the judgment to come. O my dear friends, examine your religion. You have a great deal of it, some of you; but what of its quality? Can your religion stand the test of poverty, and scandal, and scorn? Can it stand the test of scientific sarcasm and learned contempt? Will your religion stand the test of long sickness of body and depression of spirit caused by weakness? What are you doing amid the common trials of life? Examine your faith well, since all hangs there. Some of us who have lain for weeks together, peering through the thin veil which pares us from the unseen, have been made to feel that nothing will suffice us but a promise which will answer the taunt, "Let him deliver us *now.*"[50]

---

[50] Let Him Deliver Him Now – Sermon delivered June 17th, 1888

19 – God Delivers

He trusts in God; let God deliver him now, if he desires him. For he said, 'I am the Son of God.'

(Matthew 27:43 ESV)

God does deliver those who trust in him. God's interposition for the faithful is not a dream, but a substantial reality.

"Many are the afflictions of the righteous but the Lord delivers him out of them all"[51]

All history proves the faithfulness of God. Those who trust God have been in all sorts of troubles; but they have always been delivered. Remember the multiplied and multiform trials of Job. Yet God sustained him to the end so that he did not charge God foolishly, but held fast his faith in the Most High. If ever you are called to the afflictions of Job you will also be called to the sustaining grace of Job. Some of God's servants have

---

[51] Psalm 34:19

been defeated in their testimony. They have borne faithful witness for God, but they have been rejected of men. Such was Jeremiah, who was born to a heritage of scorn from those whose benefit he sought. Yet he was delivered. He shrank not from being faithful. His courage could not be silenced. By integrity he was delivered.

Godly men have been despised and misrepresented, and yet have been delivered. Remember David and his envious brethren, David and the malignant Saul, David when his men spoke of stoning him. Yet he took off the giant's head; yet he came to the throne; yet the Lord built him a house.

Some of God's servants have been bitterly persecuted, but God has delivered them. Daniel came forth from the lions' den, and the three holy children from the midst of the burning fiery furnace. These are only one or two out of millions who trusted God and he delivered them. Out of all manner of ill the Lord delivered them. God brought this crowd of witnesses through all their trials unto his throne, where they rest with Jesus, and share the triumph of their Master at this very day. O my timid brother, nothing has happened to you but what is common to men. Your battle is not different from the warfare of the rest of the saints; and as God has delivered them he will deliver you also, seeing you put your trust in him.

But *God's ways of deliverance are his own.* He does not deliver according to the translation put upon "deliverance" by the crowd. He does not deliver according to the interpretation put upon "deliverance" by our shrinking flesh and blood. He delivers, but it is in his own way. Let me remark that, *if God delivers you and me in the same way as he delivered his own Son, we can have no cause of complaint.*

Well, what kind of a deliverance was that? Did the Father tear up the cross from the earth? Did he proceed to draw out the nails from the sacred hands and feet of his dear Son? Did he set him down upon that "green hill far away, beyond the city wall," and place in his hand a sword of fire with which to smite his adversaries? Did he bid the earth open and swallow up all his foes? No; nothing of the kind. Jehovah did not interpose to spare his Son a single pang; but he let him die. He let him be taken as a dead man down from the cross and laid in a tomb. Jesus went through with his suffering to the bitter end. O brothers and sisters, this may be God's way of delivering us. We have trusted in God that he would deliver us; and his rendering of his promise is, that he will enable us to go through with it; we shall suffer to the last, and triumph in so doing.

Yet God's way of delivering those who trust in him is *always the best way.* If the Father had taken his Son down from the cross, what would have been the result? Redemption unaccomplished, salvation work undone, and Jesus returning with his life-work unfinished. This would not have been deliverance, but defeat. It was much better for our Lord Jesus to die. Now he has paid the ransom for his elect, and having accomplished the great purpose of atonement, he has slept a while in the heart of the earth, and now has ascended to his throne in the endless glories of heaven. It was deliverance of the fullest kind; for from the pangs of his death has come the joy of life to his redeemed. It is not God's will that every mountain should be levelled, but that we should be the stronger for climbing the difficult hill. God will deliver; he must deliver, but he will do it in our cases, as in the case of our Lord, in the best possible manner.

Some of you are the children of God, but you are in peculiar trouble. Well, what are you going to do? You have always trusted in God before; are you going to doubt him now? "O my dear sir, you do not know my distress; I am the most afflicted person in the church." Be it so; but you trusted in the Lord the past twenty years, and I do not believe that you have seen any just cause for denying him your confidence now. The Lord will deliver you even now. Do not let us suppose that we have come where boundless love and infinite wisdom cannot reach us. Do not fancy that you have leaped upon a ledge of rock so high as to be out of reach of the everlasting arm. If you had done so I would still cry—Throw yourself down into the arms of God, and trust that he will not let you be destroyed.[52]

---

[52] Let Him Deliver Him Now – Sermon delivered June 17th, 1888

20 – The Dying Thief

And he said, "Jesus, remember me when you come into your kingdom." And he said to him, "Truly, I say to you, today you will be with me in paradise."

(Luke 23:42-43 ESV)

The story of the salvation of the dying thief is a standing instance of the power of Christ to save, and of his abundant willingness to receive all that come to him, in whatever plight they may be. I cannot regard this act of grace as a solitary instance, any more than the salvation of Zacchaeus, the restoration of Peter, or the call of Saul, the persecutor.

Every conversion is, in a sense, singular: no two are exactly alike, and yet any one conversion is a type of others. The case of the dying thief is much more similar to our conversion than it is dissimilar; in point of fact, his case may be regarded as typical, rather than as an extraordinary incident. So I shall use it at this time. May the Holy Spirit speak through it to the encouragement of those who are ready to despair!

Remember, beloved friends, that our Lord Jesus, at the time he saved this malefactor, was at his lowest. His glory had been ebbing out in Gethsemane, and before Caiaphas, and Herod, and Pilate; but it had now reached the utmost low-water mark. Stripped of his garments, and nailed to the cross, our Lord was mocked by a crowd, and was dying in agony: then was he "numbered with the transgressors"[53]. Yet, while in that condition, he achieved this marvellous deed of grace. Behold the wonder wrought by the Saviour when emptied of all his glory, and hanged up a spectacle of shame upon the brink of death! How certain is it that he can do great wonders of mercy now, seeing that he has returned unto his glory, and sits upon the throne of light?

"He is able to save completely those who come to God through him, because he always lives to intercede for them"[54] If a dying Saviour saved the thief, he can do even

---

[53] Isaiah 53:12
[54] Hebrews 7:25

more now that he lives and reigns. All power is given unto him in heaven and in earth; can anything at this present time surpass the power of his grace?

It is not only the weakness of our Lord which makes the salvation of the penitent thief memorable; it is the fact that the dying malefactor saw it before his very eyes. Can you put yourself into his place, and suppose yourself to be looking upon one who hangs in agony upon a cross? Could you readily believe him to be the Lord of glory, who would soon come to his kingdom? That was no mean faith which, at such a moment, could believe in Jesus as Lord and King. If the apostle Paul were here, and wanted to add a New Testament chapter to the eleventh of Hebrews, he might certainly commence his instances of remarkable faith with this thief, who believed in a crucified, derided, and dying Christ, and cried to him as to one whose kingdom would surely come.

The thief's faith was the more remarkable because he was himself in great pain, and bound to die. It is not easy to exercise confidence when you are tortured with deadly anguish. Our own peace of mind has, at times, been greatly hindered by bodily pain. When we are the subjects of acute suffering it is not easy to exhibit that faith which we think we possess at other times. This man, suffering as he did, and seeing the Saviour in so sad a state, nevertheless believed unto life eternal. This kind of faith as is seldom seen.

Recollect, also, that he was surrounded by scoffers. It is easy to swim with the current, and hard to go against the stream. This man heard the priests, in their pride, ridicule the Lord, and the great multitude of the common people, with one consent, joined in the scorning; his comrade caught the spirit of the hour, and mocked also, and perhaps he did the same for a while; but through the grace of God he was changed, and believed in the Lord Jesus in the teeth of all the scorn.

His faith was not affected by his surroundings; but he, dying thief as he was, made sure his confidence. Like a jutting rock, standing out in the midst of a torrent, he declared the innocence of the Christ whom others blasphemed. His faith is worthy of our imitation in its fruits. He had no member that was free except his tongue, and he used that member wisely to rebuke his fellow criminal, and defend his Lord. His faith brought forth a brave testimony and a bold confession. I am not going to praise the thief, or his faith, but to extol the glory of that grace divine which gave the thief such faith, and then freely saved him by its means.

I am anxious to show how glorious the Saviour is — that Saviour who, at such a time, could save such a man, and give him so great a faith, and so perfectly and speedily prepare him for eternal bliss. Behold the power of that divine Spirit who could produce such faith on soil so unlikely, and in a climate so unpropitious.[55]

---

[55] The Believing Thief – Sermon delivered April 7th, 1889

21 – The Last Companion

And he said, "Jesus, remember me when you come into your kingdom." And he said to him, "Truly, I say to you, today you will be with me in paradise."

(Luke 23:42-43 ESV)

The crucified thief was our Lord's last companion on Earth. What sorry company our Lord selected when he was here! He did not consort with the religious Pharisees but he was known as "the friend of tax collectors and sinners"[56].

How I rejoice at this! It gives me assurance that he will not refuse to associate with *me.* When the Lord Jesus made a friend of me, he certainly did not make a choice which brought him credit. Do you think he gained any honour when he made a friend of you? Has he ever gained anything by us? No!

---

[56] Luke 7:34

We are thankful that he came "not to call the righteous, but sinners to repentance"[57]. As the great physician, our Lord was much with the sick: he went where there was room for him to exercise his healing care. The whole have no need of a physician: they cannot appreciate him, nor afford scope for his skill; and therefore he did not frequent their abodes.

Our Lord did make a good choice when he saved you and me; for in us he has found abundant room for his mercy and grace. There has been elbow room for his love to work within the awful emptiness of our necessities and sins; and therein he has done great things for us.

The person who believed upon the cross was a convict, who had lain in the condemned cell, and was then undergoing execution for his crimes. A convicted felon was the person with whom our Lord last consorted upon earth. What a lover of the souls of guilty men is he! What a stoop he makes to the very lowest of mankind! To this most unworthy of men the Lord of glory spoke with matchless

---

[57] Luke 5:32

grace. He spoke to him such wondrous words as never can be excelled if you search the Scriptures through: "To-day shalt you be with me in paradise." None of you are excluded from the infinite mercy of Christ, however great your iniquity: if you believe in Jesus, he will save *you.*

I do not suppose that this man had seriously thought of the Lord Jesus before. Yet, now, all of a sudden, he wakes up to the conviction that the man who is dying at his side is something more than a man. He reads the title over his head, and believes it to be true—"This is Jesus the King of the Jews." Do you see this truth, that the moment a man knows Jesus to be the Christ of God he may at once put his trust in him and be saved?

A certain preacher said, "Do you, who have been living in sin for fifty years, believe that you can in a moment be made clean through the blood of Jesus?" I answer, "Yes! We do believe that in one moment, through the precious blood of Jesus, the blackest soul can be made white. We do believe that in a single instant the sins of sixty or seventy years can be absolutely forgiven, and that the old nature, which has gone on growing worse and worse, can receive its death-wound in a moment of time, while the life eternal may be implanted in the soul at once."

This man had reached the end of his tether, but all of a sudden he woke up to the assured conviction that the Messiah was at his side, and, believing, he looked to him and lived.

I constantly meet with persons in this condition: they have lived a life of wantonness, excess, and carelessness, and they begin to feel the fire-flakes of the tempest of wrath falling upon their flesh; they dwell in an earthly hell, a prelude of eternal woe. Remorse, like an asp, has stung them, and set their blood on fire: they cannot rest, they are troubled day and night. "Be sure your sin will find you out"[58]. It has found them out, and arrested them, and they feel the strong grip of conviction. This man was in that horrible condition: the crucifixion was sure to be fatal; in a short time his legs would be broken, to end his wretched existence. He, poor soul, had but a short time to live — only the space between

---

[58] Numbers 32:23

noon and sundown; but it was long enough for the Saviour, who is mighty to save. This is the glory of Christ's grace.

This man whom Christ saved was a man who could do no good works. If salvation had been by good works, he could not have been saved; for he was fastened hand and foot to the tree of doom. It was all over with him as to any act or deed of righteousness. He could say a good word or two, but that was all; he could perform no acts; and if his salvation had depended on an active life of usefulness, certainly he never could have been saved. He was a sinner also, who could not exhibit a long-enduring repentance for sin, for he had so short a time to live. He could not have experienced bitter convictions, lasting over months and years, for his time was measured by moments, and he was on the borders of the grave. His end was very near, and yet the Saviour could save him, and did save him so perfectly, that the sun went not down till he was in paradise with Christ.[59]

---

[59] The Believing Thief – Sermon delivered April 7th, 1889

22 – Companion in Paradise

And he said, "Jesus, remember me when you come into your kingdom." And he said to him, "Truly, I say to you, today you will be with me in paradise."

(Luke 23:42-43 ESV)

This man was our Lord's companion at the gate of paradise.

Who is this that enters the pearl-gate at the same moment as the King of glory? Who is this favoured companion of the Redeemer? Is it some honoured martyr? Is it a faithful apostle? Is it a patriarch, like Abraham; or a prince, like David? It is none of these. Behold, and be amazed at sovereign grace. He that goes in at the gate of paradise, with the King of glory, is a thief! He is saved in no inferior way, and received into bliss in no secondary style.

I think the Saviour took him with him as a specimen of what he meant to do. He seemed to say to all the heavenly powers, "I bring a sinner with me; he is a sample of the rest."

Jesus said, "Today you shall be with me in paradise." Paradise means a garden, a garden filled with delights. The garden of Eden is the type of heaven. Our Saviour took this dying thief into the paradise of infinite delight, and this is where he will take all of us sinners who believe in him. If we are trusting him, we shall ultimately be with him in paradise.

If the Lord said, "Today you shall be *with me,*" we should not need him to add another word; for where he is, is heaven to us. He added the word "paradise," because otherwise no one could have guessed where he was going. Think of it; you are to dwell with the altogether-lovely One for ever. You poor and needy ones, you are to be with him in his glory, in his bliss, in his perfection. Where he is, and as he is, you shall be. The Lord looks into those weeping eyes of yours this morning, and he says, "Poor sinner, you shall one day be with me." I think I hear you say, "Lord, that is bliss too great for such a sinner as I am"; but he replies — I have loved you with an everlasting love: therefore with lovingkindness will I draw you, till you shall be with me where I am.

"Today!" You shalt not lie in purgatory for ages, nor sleep in limbo for many years; but you shalt be ready for bliss at once, and at once you shall enjoy it. The sinner was hard by the gates of hell, but almighty mercy lifted him up, and the Lord said, "*Today* you shall be with me in paradise." What a change from the cross to the crown, from the anguish of Calvary to the glory of the New Jerusalem! In those few hours the beggar was lifted from the dunghill and set among princes.

Can you measure the change from that sinner, loathsome in his iniquity, when the sun was high at noon, to that same sinner, clothed in pure white, and accepted in the Beloved, in the paradise of God, when the sun went down? O glorious Saviour, what marvels you can work! How rapidly you work them!

Notice *the certainty of it.* He says, "Truly." Our blessed Lord on the cross returned to his old majestic manner, as he painfully turned his head, and looked on his convert. He often began his preaching with, "Truly, truly, I say unto you"; and now that he is dying he uses his favourite manner, and says, "Truly." Our Lord took no oath; his strongest asseveration was, "Truly, truly." To give the penitent the plainest assurance, he says, "Truly I say unto you, today you shall be with me in paradise." In this he had an absolutely indisputable assurance that though he must die, yet he would live and find himself in paradise with his Lord.

Why should not you and I pass through that pearl-gate in due time, clothed in his merit, washed in his blood, resting on his power? One of these days angels will say of you, and of me, "Who is this that cometh up from the wilderness, leaning upon her beloved?"[60]

The shining ones will be amazed to see some of us coming. If you have lived a life of sin until now, but repent and enter heaven, what an amazement there will be in every golden street to think that you have come there!

The salvation of this convicted highwayman has made our Lord illustrious for mercy even

---

[60] Song of Songs 8:5

unto this day; would not your case do the same? Would not saints cry, "Hallelujah! Hallelujah!" if they heard that some of you had been turned from darkness to marvellous light? Why should it not be? Believe in Jesus, and it is so.[61]

---

[61] The Believing Thief – Sermon delivered April 7th, 1889

23 – The Lord's Sermon to Us

And he said, "Jesus, remember me when you come into your kingdom." And he said to him, "Truly, I say to you, today you will be with me in paradise."

(Luke 23:42-43 ESV)

Satan asks to come to the front and preach to you; whispering, "You see you can be saved at the very last. Put off repentance and faith; you may be forgiven on your death-bed."

Abhor his deceitful teaching. Do not be ungrateful because God is kind. Do not provoke the Lord because he is patient. Such conduct would be unworthy and ungrateful. Do not run an awful risk because one escaped the tremendous peril. The Lord will accept all who repent; but how do you know that you will repent? It is true that one thief was saved—but the other thief was lost. One is saved, and we may not despair; the other is lost, and we may not presume. Dear friends, I trust you are not made of such diabolical stuff as to fetch from the mercy of God an argument for continuing in sin. If you do, I can only say of you, your damnation will be just; you will have brought it upon yourselves.

Consider now the teaching of our Lord; He is ready to save at the last moment. He was just passing away; his foot was on the doorstep of the Father's house. Up comes this poor sinner the last thing at night, at the eleventh hour, and the Saviour smiles and declares that he will not enter except with this belated wanderer. At the very gate he declares that this seeking soul shall enter with him. There was plenty of time for him to have come before: you know how apt we are to say, "You have waited to the last moment. I am just going off, and I cannot attend to you now."

Our Lord had his dying pangs upon him, and yet he attends to the perishing criminal, and permits him to pass through the heavenly portal in his company. Jesus loves to rescue sinners from going down into the pit. You will be very happy if you are saved, but you will not be one half so happy as he will be when he saves you.

He comes to us full of tenderness, with tears in his eyes, mercy in his hands, and love in his heart. You shall find your transgressions put away, and your sins pardoned once for all, if you now trust him.

This man believed that Jesus was the Christ. The next thing he did was to say, "Lord, remember me." Jesus might have said, "What have I to do with you, and what have you to do with me? What has a thief to do with the perfect One?" Many of you, good people, try to get as far away as you can from the erring and fallen. They might infect your innocence! Society claims that we should not be familiar with people who have offended against its laws. We must not be seen associating with them, for it might discredit us. Infamous bosh! Can anything discredit sinners such as we are by nature and by practice?

If we know ourselves before God we are degraded enough in and of ourselves? Is there anybody, after all, in the world, who is worse than we are when we see ourselves in the faithful glass of the Word? As soon as ever a man believes that Jesus is the Christ, let him hook himself on to him. The moment you believe Jesus to be the Saviour, seize upon him as your Saviour.

Jesus is the common property of all sinners who make bold to take him. Every sinner who has the will to do so may take the Lord home with him.

Heaven and hell are not places far away. You may be in heaven before the clock ticks again, it is so near. It is all there, and all near. "Today," said the Lord; within three or four hours at the longest, "shalt you be with me in paradise;" so near is it. We are all within measurable distance of heaven or hell. Oh, that we, instead of trifling about such things, because they seem so far away, would solemnly realize them, since they are so very near! This very day, before the sun goes down, some hearer, now sitting in this place, may see, in his own spirit, the realities of heaven or hell.

Furthermore, know that *if you have believed in Jesus you are prepared for heaven.* It may be that you will have to live on earth twenty, or thirty, or forty years to glorify Christ; and, if so, be thankful for the privilege; but if you do not live another hour, your instantaneous death would not alter the fact that he that believes in the Son of God is fit for heaven. Surely, if anything beyond faith is needed to make us fit to enter paradise, the thief would have been kept a little longer here; but no, he is, in the morning, in the state of nature, at noon he enters the state of grace, and by sunset he is in the state of glory.

I read somewhere, and I think it is true, that some ministers preach the gospel in the same way as donkeys eat thistles, namely, very, very cautiously. On the contrary, I will preach it boldly. I have not the slightest alarm about the matter. If any of you misuse free-grace teaching, I cannot help it. He that will be damned can as well ruin himself by perverting the gospel as by anything else.

If the Saviour had meant this to be a solitary case, he would have faintly said to him, "Do not let anybody know; but you shall to day be in the kingdom with me." No, our Lord spoke openly, and those about him heard what he said. The Saviour had this wonder of grace reported in the daily news of the gospel, because he means to repeat the marvel every day.

I pray you, therefore, if any of you have not yet trusted in my Lord Jesus, come and trust in him now. Trust him wholly; trust him only; trust him at once. Then will you sing with me:

"The dying thief rejoiced to see
That fountain in his day,
And there have I, though vile as he,
Washed all my sins away"[62] [63]

---

[62] There is a fountain filled with blood, William Cowper
[63] The Believing Thief – Sermon delivered April 7th, 1889

24 – The Depth of Grief

And about the ninth hour Jesus cried out
with a loud voice, saying, *"Eli, Eli, lema
sabachthani?"* that is, *"My God, my God,
why have you forsaken me?"*

(Matthew 27:46 ESV)

"There was darkness over all the land unto
the ninth hour"[64]

Jesus' cry came out of that darkness. Expect
not to see through its every word, as though
it came from on high as a beam from the
unclouded Sun of Righteousness. There is
light in it, bright, flashing light: but there is a
centre of impenetrable gloom, where the
soul is ready to faint because of the terrible
darkness.

---

[64] Matthew 27:45

Our Lord was then in the darkest pare of his way. He had trodden the winepress now for hours, and the work was almost finished. He had reached the culminating point of his anguish. This is his lament from the lowest pit of misery—"My God, my God, why have you forsaken me?" I do not think that the records of time or even of eternity, contain a sentence more full of anguish.

Here the wormwood and the gall, and all the other bitterness, are outdone. Here you may look as into a vast abyss; and though you strain your eyes, and gaze until sight fails you, yet you perceive no bottom; it is measureless, unfathomable, inconceivable. This anguish of the Saviour on your behalf and mine is no more to be measured and weighed than the sin which needed it, or the love which endured it. We will adore where we cannot comprehend.

You shall measure the height of his love, if it be ever measured, by the depth of his grief, if that can ever be known. See with what a price he has redeemed us from the curse of the law! As you see this, say to yourselves: What manner of people ought we to be! What measure of love ought we to return to one who bore the utmost penalty, that we might he delivered from the wrath to come? I do not profess that I can dive into this deep: I will only venture to the edge of the precipice, and bid you look down, and pray the Spirit of God to concentrate your mind upon this lamentation of our dying Lord, as it rises up through the thick darkness.

God had forsaken him. Grief of mind is harder to bear than pain of body. You can pluck up courage and endure the pang of sickness and pain, so long as the spirit is brave; but if the soul itself be touched, and the mind becomes diseased with anguish, then every pain is increased in severity, and there is nothing with which to sustain it. Spiritual sorrows are the worst of mental miseries.

A man may bear great depression of spirit about worldly matters, if he feels that he has his God to go to. He is cast down, but not in despair. Like David, he dialogues with himself, and he enquires, "Why are you cast down, O my soul? Hope you in God: for I shall yet praise him"[65] But if the Lord be once

---

[65] Psalm 43:5

withdrawn, if the comfortable light of his presence be shadowed even for an hour, there is a torment within the breast, which I can only liken to the prelude of hell. This is the greatest of all weights that can press upon the heart. This made the Psalmist plead, "Hide not your face from me; put not your servant away in anger"[66] We can bear a bleeding body, and even a wounded spirit; but a soul conscious of desertion by God it beyond conception unendurable. When he holds back the face of his throne, and spreads his cloud upon it, who can endure the darkness?

I have done my best, but I seem to myself to have been prattling like a little child, talking about something infinitely above me. So, I leave the solemn fact, that our Lord Jesus was on the tree forsaken of his God.[67]

---

[66] Psalm 27:9

[67] Lama Sabachthani? – Sermon delivered March 2nd, 1890

25 – The Fact of Suffering

And about the ninth hour Jesus cried out
with a loud voice, saying, *"Eli, Eli, lema
sabachthani?"* that is, *"My God, my God,
why have you forsaken me?"*

(Matthew 27:46 ESV)

This forsaking was *very terrible.* Who can
fully tell what it is to be forsaken of God? We
can only form a guess by what we have
ourselves felt under temporary and partial
desertion. God has never left us, altogether;
for he has expressly said, "I will never leave
you, nor forsake you"[68]; yet we have
sometimes felt as if he had cast us off. Thus
we are able to form some little idea of how
the Saviour felt when his God had forsaken
him.

The mind of Jesus was left to dwell upon one
dark subject, and no cheering theme

---

[68] Deuteronomy 31:6

consoled him. It was the hour in which he was made to stand before God as consciously the sin-bearer, according to that ancient prophecy, "He shall bear their iniquities"[69] Then was it true, "He has made him to be sin for us"[70]. Peter puts it, "He bore our sins in his own body on the tree"[71]

Sin, sin, sin was everywhere around and about Christ. He had no sin of his own; but the Lord had "laid on him the iniquity of us all"[72] He had no strength given him from on high, no secret oil and wine poured into his wounds; but he was made to appear in the lone character of the Lamb of God, who takes away the sin of the world; and therefore he must feel the weight of sin, and the turning away of that sacred face which cannot look upon sin.

His Father, at that time, gave him no open acknowledgment. On certain other occasions a voice had been heard, saying,

---

[69] Isaiah 53:11
[70] 2 Corinthians 5:21
[71] 1 Peter 2:24
[72] Isaiah 53:6

"This is my beloved Son, in whom I am well pleased"[73]; but now, when such a testimony seemed most of all required, the oracle was dumb. He was hung up as an accursed thing upon the cross; for he was "made a curse for us, as it is written, Cursed is every one that hangs on a tree"[74]; and the Lord his God did not own him before men.

I remember, also, that our blessed Lord had lived in unbroken fellowship with God, and to be forsaken was a new grief to him. He had never known what the dark was until then: his life had been lived in the light of God. Think, dear child of God, if you had always dwelt in full communion with God, your days would have been as the days of heaven upon earth; and how cold it would strike to your heart to find yourself in the darkness of desertion. If you can conceive such a thing as happening to a perfect man, you can see why to Jesus it was a special trial. Remember, he had enjoyed fellowship with God more richly, as well as more constantly, than any of us. His fellowship with the Father

---

[73] Luke 3:22
[74] Galatians 3:13

was of the highest, deepest, fullest order; and what must the loss of it have been?

A sinful man has an awful need of God, but he does not know it; and therefore he does not feel that hunger and thirst after God which would come upon a perfect man could he be deprived of God. The very perfection of his nature renders it inevitable that the holy man must either be in communion with God, or be desolate.

Our Lord's heart, and all his nature were, morally and spiritually, so delicately formed, so sensitive, so tender, that to be without God, was to him a grief which could not be weighed. I see him in the text bearing desertion, and yet I perceive that he cannot bear it. I know not how to express my meaning except by such a paradox. He cannot endure to be without God. He had surrendered himself to be left of God, as the representative of sinners must be, but his pure and holy nature, after three hours of silence, finds the position unendurable to love and purity; and breaking forth from it, now that the hour was over, he exclaims, "Why have you forsaken me?" He quarrels not with the suffering, but he cannot abide in the position which caused it. He seems as if he must end the ordeal, not because of the pain, but because of the moral shock. We have here the repetition after his passion of that loathing which he felt before it, when he cried, "If it be possible let this cup pass from me: nevertheless not as I will, but as you will" [75]

"My God, my God, why have you forsaken me?" is the holiness of Christ amazed at the position of substitute for guilty men.[76]

---

[75] Matthew 26:39
[76] Lama Sabachthani? – Sermon delivered March 2nd, 1890

26 – The Enquiry

And about the ninth hour Jesus cried out
with a loud voice, saying, *"Eli, Eli, lema
sabachthani?"* that is, *"My God, my God,
why have you forsaken me?"*

(Matthew 27:46 ESV)

Note carefully Jesus' cry—"My God, my
God, why have you forsaken me?" It is pure
anguish, undiluted agony, which cries like
this; but it is the agony of a godly soul; for
only a man of that order would have used
such an expression. Let us learn from it
useful lessons.

This cry is taken from the Bible. Does it not
show our Lord's love of the sacred volume,
that when he felt his sharpest grief, he
turned to the Scripture to find a fit utterance
for it? Here we have the opening sentence of
the twenty-second Psalm. Oh, that we may
so love the inspired Word that we may not
only sing to its score, but even weep to its
music!

Note, again, that our Lord's lament is an address to God. The godly, in their anguish, turn to the hand which smites them. The Saviour's outcry is not *against* God, but *to* God. "My God, my God": he makes a double effort to draw near. True Sonship is here. The child in the dark is crying after his Father—"My God, my God." Both the Bible and prayer were dear to Jesus in his agony.

Still, observe, it is a faith-cry; for though it asks, "Why have you forsaken me?" yet it first says, twice over, "My God, my God." The grip of appropriation is in the word "my"; but the reverence of humility is in the word "God." It is "'My *God,* my *God,*' you are God forever to me, and I a poor creature. I do not quarrel with you. Your rights are unquestioned, for you are my *God.* You can do as you will, and I yield to your sacred sovereignty. I kiss the hand that smites me, and with all my heart I cry, 'My God, my God.'" When you are delirious with pain, think of your Bible still: when your mind wanders, let it roam towards the mercy seat; and when your heart and your flesh fail, still live by faith, and still cry, "My God, my God."

The one Mediator between God and man, the man Christ Jesus, beheld the holiness of God in arms against the sin of man, whose nature he had espoused. God was for him and with him in a certain unquestionable sense; but for the time, so far as his feeling went, God was against him, and necessarily withdrawn from him. It is not surprising that the holy soul of Christ should shudder at finding itself brought into painful contact with the infinite justice of God, even though its design was only to vindicate that justice, and glorify the Law-giver. Our Lord could now say, "All your waves and your billows have gone over me"[77] and therefore he uses language which is all too hot with anguish to be dissected by the cold hand of a logical criticism.

Do you not think that *the amazement of our Lord, when he was "made sin for us"[78]* , led him to cry out like this? For such a sacred and pure being to be made a sin-offering was an amazing experience. Sin was laid on him, and he was treated as if he had been guilty, though he had personally never sinned; and

---

[77] Psalm 42:7
[78] 2 Corinthians 5:21

now the infinite horror of rebellion against the most holy God fills his holy soul, the unrighteousness of sin breaks his heart, and he stares back from it, crying, "My God, my God, why have you forsaken *me?*" Why must I bear the dread result of contact I so much abhor?

Think, for a moment, that the Lord God, in the broadest and most unreserved sense, could never, in very deed, have forsaken his most obedient Son. He was ever with him in the grand design of salvation. Towards the Lord Jesus, personally, God himself, personally, must ever have stood on terms of infinite love. Truly the Only Begotten was never more lovely to the Father than when he was obedient unto death, even the death of the cross! But we must look upon God here as the Judge of all the earth, and we must look upon the Lord Jesus also in his official capacity, as the Surety of the covenant, and the sacrifice for sin.

The great Judge of all cannot smile upon him who has become the substitute for the guilty. Sin is loathed of God; and if, in order to its removal his own Son is made to bear it, yet, as sin, it is still loathsome, and he who bears it cannot be in happy communion with God. This was the dreaded necessity of expiation; but in the essence of things the love of the great Father to his Son never ceased, nor ever knew a diminution. Restrained in its flow it must be, but lessened at its fountain-head it could not be. [79]

[79] Lama Sabachthani? – Sermon delivered March 2nd, 1890

27 – The Answer

> And about the ninth hour Jesus cried out
> with a loud voice, saying, *"Eli, Eli, lema
> sabachthani?"* that is, *"My God, my God,
> why have you forsaken me?"*

> (Matthew 27:46 ESV)

What is the outcome of this suffering? What was the reason for it? Our Saviour could answer his own question. If for a moment his manhood was perplexed, yet his mind soon came to clear apprehension; for he said, "It is finished"; and he then referred to the work which in his lonely agony he had been performing. Why, then, did God forsake his Son? I cannot conceive any other answer than this—*he stood in our stead.* There was no reason in Christ why the Father should forsake him: he was perfect, and his life was without spot.

God never acts without reason; and since there were no reasons in the character and person of the Lord Jesus why his Father should forsake him, we must look elsewhere.

"Yet all the griefs he felt were ours,
Ours were the woes he bore;
Pangs, not his own, his spotless soul
With bitter anguish tore.

"We held him as condemned of heaven,
An outcast from his God;
While for our sins he groaned, he bled,
Beneath his Father's rod."[80]

He bore the sinner's sin, and he had to be treated, therefore, as though he were a sinner, though sinner be could never be. With his own full consent he suffered as though he had committed the transgressions which were laid on him. Our sin, and his taking it upon himself, is the answer to the question, "Why have you forsaken me?"

We now see that *His obedience was perfect.* He came into the world to obey the Father, and he rendered that obedience to the very uttermost. The spirit of obedience could go no farther than for one who feels forsaken of God still to cling to him in

---

[80] How few receive with cordial faith, Thomas Haweis

solemn, avowed allegiance, still declaring before a mocking multitude his confidence in the afflicting God. It is noble to cry, "My God, my God," when one is asking, "Why have you forsaken me?" How much farther can obedience go? I see nothing beyond it. The soldier at the gate of Pompeii remaining at his post as sentry when the shower of burning ashes is falling, was not more true to his trust than he who adheres to a forsaking God with loyalty of hope.

He must feel forsaken of God because this is the necessary consequence of sin. For a man to be forsaken of God is the penalty which naturally and inevitably follows upon his breaking his relation with God. What is death? What was the death that was threatened to Adam? "On the day that you eat of the tree you shall surely die"[81]

Is death annihilation? Was Adam annihilated that day? Assuredly not: he lived many a year afterwards. But in the day in which he ate of the forbidden fruit he died by being separated from God. The separation of the soul from God is spiritual death; just as the

---

[81] Genesis 3:17

separation of the soul from the body is natural death. The sacrifice for sin must be put in the place of separation, and must bow to the penalty of death. By this placing of the Great Sacrifice under forsaking and death, it would be seen by all creatures throughout the universe that God could not have fellowship with sin. If even the Holy One, who stood the Just for the unjust, found God forsaking him, what must the doom of the actual sinner be! Sin is evidently always, in every case, a dividing influence, putting even the Christ himself, as a sin-bearer, in the place of distance.

Let us lean hard, let us bear with all our weight on our Lord. He will bear the full weight of all our sin and care. As to my sin, I hear its harsh accusations no more when I hear Jesus cry, "Why have you forsaken me?" I know that I deserve the deepest hell at the hand of God's vengeance; but I am not afraid. He will never forsake *me,* for he forsook his Son on my behalf. I shall not suffer for my sin, for Jesus has suffered to the full in my stead.

Behind this brazen wall of substitution a sinner is safe. These "munitions of rock" guard all believers, and they may rest secure. The rock is cleft for me; I hide in its rifts, and no harm can reach me. You have a full atonement, a great sacrifice, a glorious vindication of the law; wherefore rest at peace, all you that put your trust in Jesus.

Let us abhor the sin which brought such agony upon our beloved Lord. What an accursed thing is sin, which crucified the Lord Jesus! Do you laugh at it? Will you go and spend an evening to see a mimic performance of it? Do you roll sin under your tongue as a sweet morsel, and then come to God's house, on the Lord's-day morning, and think to worship him?

Worship him! Worship him, with sin indulged in your breast! Worship him, with sin loved and pampered in your life! If I had a dear brother who had been murdered, what would you think of me if I valued the knife which had been crimsoned with his blood? Sin murdered Christ; will you be a friend to it? Sin pierced the heart of the Incarnate God; can you love it? Oh, that there was an abyss as deep as Christ's misery, that I might at once hurl this dagger of sin into its depths, whence it might never be brought to light again! Begone, O sin! You are banished from the heart where Jesus reigns! Begone, for you have crucified my Lord, and made him cry, "Why have you forsaken me?" O my hearers, if you did but know yourselves, and know the love of Christ, you would each one vow that you would harbour sin no longer. You would be indignant at sin, and cry,

> "The dearest idol I have known,
> Whate'er that idol be,
> Lord, I will tear it from its throne,
> And worship only you"[82] [83]

---

[82] O for a closer walk with God, William Cowper
[83] Lama Sabachthani? – Sermon delivered March 2nd, 1890

28 – Turning to God

And about the ninth hour Jesus cried out
with a loud voice, saying, *"Eli, Eli, lema
sabachthani?"* that is, *"My God, my God,
why have you forsaken me?"*

(Matthew 27:46 ESV)

At that time when he uttered these words,
God had left him to his enemies. No angel
appeared to interpose and destroy the
power of Roman or Jew. He seemed utterly
given up. The people might mock at him, and
they might put him to what pain they
pleased just at the same time a sense of
God's love to him as man was taken from
him. The comfortable presence of God,
which had all his life long sustained him,
began to withdraw from him in the garden,
and appeared to be quite gone when he was
just in the article of death upon the cross;
and meanwhile the waves of God's wrath on
account of sin began to break over his spirit,
and he was in the condition of a soul
deserted by God.

Now sometimes believers come into the same condition, not to the same extent, but in a measure. Yesterday they were full of joy, for the love of God was shed abroad in their hearts, but to-day that sense of love is gone; they droop; they feel heavy. Now the temptation will be at such times for them to sit down and look into their own hearts; and if they do, they will grow more wretched every moment, until they will come close to despair; for there is no comfort to be found within, when there is no light from above.

Our signs and tokens within are like sundials. We can tell what is o'clock by the sundial when the sun shines, but if it does not what is the use of the sundial? And so marks of evidence may help us when God's love is shed abroad in the soul, but when that is done, marks of evidence stand us in very little stead.

Now observe our Lord. He is deserted of God, but instead of looking in, and saying, "My soul, why are you this? Why are you that? Why are you cast down? Why do you mourn?" he looks straight away from that dried-up well that is within, to those eternal waters that never can be stopped, and which are always full of refreshment. He cries, "My God." He knows which way to look, and I say to every Christian here, it is a temptation of the devil, when you are desponding, and when you are not enjoying your religion as you did, to begin peering and searching about in the dunghill of your own corruptions, and stirring over all that you are feeling, and all you ought to feel, and all you do not feel, and all that. Instead of that look from within, look above, look to your God again, for the light will come there.

And you will notice that *our Lord did not at this time look to any of his friends.* In the beginning of his sufferings he appeared to seek consolation from his disciples, but he found them sleeping for sorrow; therefore, on this occasion he did not look to them in any measure.

He had lost the light or God's countenance, but he does not look down in the darkness and say, "John, dear faithful John, are you there? Have you not a word for him whose bosom was a pillow for your head? Mother Mary, are you there? Can you not say one soft word to your dying son to let him know there is still a one that does not forget him?"

No, our Lord did not look to the creature. Man as he was, and we must regard him as such in uttering this cry, yet he does not look to friend or brother, helper or human arm.

Even if God seems to forsake you, keep on crying to him. Do not begin to look in a pet and a jealous humour to creatures, but still look to your God. Depend upon it, he will come to you sooner or later. He cannot fail you. He must help you. Like a child if its mother strike it, still if it be in pain it cries for its mother; it knows her love; it knows its deep need of her, and that she alone can supply its need. Oh! Beloved, do the same. Is there one in this house who has lately lost his comforts, and Satan has said, "Don't pray"? Beloved, pray more than ever you did. If the devil says, "Why, God is angry; what is the use of praying to him?" he might have said the same to Christ—"Why do you pray to one who forsakes you?" But Christ did pray "My God"

Perhaps Satan tells you not to read the Bible again. It has not comforted you of late; the promises have not come to your soul. Dear brother, read and read more; read double as much as ever you did. Do not think that, because there is no light coming to you, the wisest way is to get away from the light. No; stay where the light is. And perhaps he even says to you, "Don't attend the house of God again; don't go to the communion table. Why, surely you won't wish to commune with God when he hides his face from you." I say the words of wisdom, for I speak according to the example of Christ; come still to your God in private and in public worship, and come still, dear brother, to the table of fellowship with Jesus, saying, "Though he slay me, vet will I trust in him" [84]

My eye shall not look to my soul, my friends, or my feelings, but I will look to my God and to him alone. [85]

---

[84] Job 13:15
[85] Our Lord's Solemn Enquiry – Sermon delivered April 7th, 1872

29 – No Relaxing His Hold

And about the ninth hour Jesus cried out
with a loud voice, saying, *"Eli, Eli, lema
sabachthani?"* that is, *"My God, my God,
why have you forsaken me?"*

(Matthew 27:46 ESV)

Though he felt deserted, Jesus did not relax
his hold on God.

He cries "My God." He believes that God is
still his God. He uses the possessive particle
twice, *"My* God, *my* God."

It is easy to believe that God is ours when he
smiles upon us, and when we have the sweet
fellowship of his love in our hearts; but the
point for faith to attend to, is to hold to God
when he gives the hard words, when his
providence frowns upon you, and when
even his Spirit seems to be withdrawn from
you. Oh! Let go everything, but do not let go
of your God. If the ship be tossed and ready

to sink, and the tempest rages exceedingly, cast out the ingots, let the gold go, throw out the wheat, as Paul's companions did. Let even necessaries go, but oh! still hold to your God.

Let the Christian, when God turns away the brightness of his presence, still believe that all his strength lies in God, and that, moreover, God's power is on his side. Though it seemed to crush him, faith says, "It is a power that will not crush me. If he smite me, what will I do? I will lay hold upon his arm, and he will put strength in me. I will deal with God as Jacob did with the angel. If he wrestle with me, I will borrow strength from him, and I will wrestle still with him until I get the blessing from him." Beloved, we must neither let go of God, nor let go of our sense of his power to save us. We must hold to our possession of him, and hold to the belief that he is worth possessing, that he is God all sufficient, and that he is our God still.

Now I would like to put this personally to any tired child of God. Are you going to let go your God because you have lost his smile? Then I ask you, did you base your faith upon his smile? For if you did, you mistook the true ground of faith. The ground of a believer's confidence is not God's smile, but God's promise. It is not his temporary sunshine of his love, but his deep eternal love itself, as it reveals itself in the covenant and in the promises. The present smile of God may go, but God's promise does not go; and if you believe upon God's promise, it is just as true when God frowns as when he smiles. If you are resting upon the covenant, that covenant is as true in the dark as in the light. It stands as good when your soul is without a single gleam of consolation as when your heart is flooded with sacred bliss.

The promise is as good as ever. Christ is the same as ever; his blood is as great a plea as ever; and the oath of God is as immutable as ever. It is His love itself we must build on— not on our enjoyment of his presence, but on his faithfulness and on his truth.

If faith gives up God because he frowns, what sort of a faith was it? Can you not believe in a frowning God? Did Job turn against his God when he took away his comforts from him? No; he said, "The Lord gave, and the Lord takes away, blessed be the name of the Lord"[86] And do you not know how he put it best of all when he said, "Though he slay me, yet will I trust in him"[87]

If your faith be only a fair-weather faith, if you can only walk with God when he sandals you in silver, and smooths the path beneath your feet, what faith is this? Where didst you get it from? But the faith that can foot it with the Lord through Nebuchadnezzar's furnace of fire, and that can go walking with him through the valley of the shadow of death — this is the faith to be had and sought after, and God will grant it to us, for that was the faith that was in the heart of Christ when forsaken of God. He says, "My God."[88]

---

[86] Job 1:21

[87] Job 13:15

[88] Our Lord's Solemn Enquiry – Sermon delivered April 7th, 1872

30 – The Inquiring Voice

And about the ninth hour Jesus cried out
with a loud voice, saying, *"Eli, Eli, lema
sabachthani?"* that is, *"My God, my God,
why have you forsaken me?"*

(Matthew 27:46 ESV)

Our Lord, when he cries, cries with the
inquiring voice of a loving child.

"My God, *why,* have you forsaken me?" He
asks a question not in curiosity, but in love.
He brings loving, sorrowful
complaints. *"Why,* my God? Why? Why?"
This is a lesson to us, because we ought to
endeavour to find out why it is that God
hides himself from us. No Christian ought to
be content to live without full assurance of
faith. No believer ought to be satisfied to live
a moment without knowing to a certainty
that Christ is his, and if he does not know it,
and assurance is gone, what ought he to do?
Why, he should never be content until he has

gone to God with the question, "Why have I not this assurance? Why have I not your presence? Why is it that I cannot live once I did in the light of your countenance?"

Beloved, the answer to this question in our case will sometimes be, "You have forsaken me. You have grown cold of heart by slow degrees; and I have made you know it to make you see your backsliding, and sorrowfully repent of it."

Sometimes the answer will be, "My child, you have set up an idol in your heart. You love your child too much, your gold too much, your trade too much; and I cannot come into your soul unless I am your Lord, your love, your bridegroom, and your all."

Oh! We shall be glad to know these answers, because the moment we know them our heart will say:

"The dearest idol I have known,
Whate'er that idol be,
Help me to tear it from its throne,
And worship only you."[89]

---

[89] O for a closer walk with God, William Cowper

Sometimes the Lord's answer will be, "My child, I have gone from you for a little to try you, to see if you love me." A true lover will love on under frowns. It is only the superficial professing Christian that wants sweet meats every day, and only loves his God for what he gets out of him. The genuine believer loves him when he smites him, when he bruises him.

Then we will say, "O God, if this is why you forsake us, we will love you still, and prove to you that your grace has made our souls to hunger and thirst for you." Depend upon it, the best way to get away from trouble, or to get great help under it, is to run close in to God. In one of Quarles's[90] poems he has the picture of a man striking another with a great nail.

Now the further off the other is, the heavier it strikes him. So the man whom God is smiting runs close in, and he cannot be hurt at all. O my God, my God, when away from you affliction stuns me, but I will close with you, and then even my affliction I will take to be a cause of glory, and glory in tribulations

---

[90] Francis Quarles

also, so that your blast shall not sorely wound my spirit.

To cry to God with the enquiry of a child is the lesson of the text. Oh! Learn it well. Do practice it when you are in much trouble. If you are in such a condition at this time, practice it now, and say, "Search me and try me, and see if there be any wicked way in me, and lead me in the way everlasting"[91] [92]

---

[91] Psalm 139:24

[92] Our Lord's Solemn Enquiry – Sermon delivered April 7th, 1872

31 – The Father's Work

And about the ninth hour Jesus cried out with a loud voice, saying, *"Eli, Eli, lema sabachthani?"* that is, *"My God, my God, why have you forsaken me?"*

(Matthew 27:46 ESV)

Our Lord, although he was forsaken, still pursued his father's work -the work he came to do.

"My God, why have you forsaken me?" But, he does not leave the cross; he does not unloose the nails as he might have done with a will; he did not leap down amidst the assembled mockers, and scorn them in return, and chase them far away. He kept on bleeding, suffering, even until he could say, "It is finished," and he did not give up the ghost till it was finished.

I find it, and I daresay you do, a very easy and pleasant thing to go on serving God when I have got a full sense of his love, and Christ shining in my face, when every text brings joy to my heart, and when I see souls converted, and know that God is going with the Word to bless it. That is very easy, but to keep on serving God when you get nothing for it but blow - when there is no success, and when your own heart is in deep darkness of spirit - I know the temptation. Perhaps you are under it. Because you have not the joy you once had, you say, "I must give up preaching; I must give up that Sunday School. If I have not the light of God's countenance, how can I do it? I must give it up." Beloved, you must do no such thing.

Suppose there were a loyal subject in a nation, and he had done something or other which grieved the king, and the king on a certain day turned his face from him, do you think that loyal subject would go away and neglect his duty because the king frowned? No; he would say to himself, "I do not know why the king seemed to deal hardly with me. He is a good king, and I know he is good, if he does not see any good in me, and I will work for him more than ever. I will prove to him that my loyalty does not depend upon his smiles. I am his loyal subject, and will stand to him still."

What would you say to your child if you had to chasten him for doing wrong, if he were to go away and say, "I shall not attend to the errand that father has sent me upon, and I shall do no more in the house that father has commanded me to do, because father has scolded me this morning"? Ah! What a disobedient child! If the discipline had its effect upon him, he would say, "I will wrong you no more, father" So let it be with us.

Besides, should not our gratitude compel us to go on working for God? Has not he saved us from hell? Then we may say, with the old heathen, "Strike, so long as you forgive." Yes, if God forgives, he may strike if he will. Suppose a judge should forgive a criminal condemned to die, but he should say to him, "Though you are not to be executed as you deserve, yet, for all that, you must be put in prison for some years," he would say, "Ah! My Lord, I will take this lesser chastisement, so long as my life is saved."

If our God has saved us from going down to the pit by putting his own Son to death on our behalf, we will love him for that, if we never have anything more. If, between here and heaven, we should have to say, like the elder brother, "You never gave me a goat that I might make merry with my friends" we will love him still; and if he never does anything to us between here and glory, but lay us on a sick bed, yet still we will praise and bless him, for he has saved us from going down to the pit; therefore, we will love him as long as we live.

Oh! if you think of God as you ought to do, you will not be at ups and downs with him, but you will serve him with all your heart, and soul, and might, whether you are enjoying the light of his countenance or not. [93]

[93] Our Lord's Solemn Enquiry – Sermon delivered April 7th, 1872

32 – A Glorious Answer

And about the ninth hour Jesus cried out
with a loud voice, saying, *"Eli, Eli, lema
sabachthani?"* that is, *"My God, my God,
why have you forsaken me?"*

(Matthew 27:46 ESV)

Jesus has received a glorious answer to his
cry.

And so shall every man that, in the same
spirit in the hour of darkness, asks the same
question. Our Lord died. No answer had
been given to the question, but the question
went on ringing through earth, and heaven,
and hell.

Three days he slept in the grave, and after a
while he went into heaven, and my
imagination, I think, may be allowed if I say
that as he entered there the echo of his
words, "Why have you forsaken me?" just
died away, and then the Father gave him the

practical answer to the question; for there, all along the golden streets, stood white-robed bands, all of them singing their redeemer's praise, all of them chanting the name of Jehovah and the Lamb; and this was a part of the answer to his question.

God had forsaken Christ that these chosen spirits might live through him; they were the reward for the travail of his soul; they were the answer to his question; and ever since then, between heaven and earth, there has been constant commerce. If your eyes were opened that you could see, you would perceive in the sky not falling stars, shooting downwards, but stars rising upward from England, many every hour from America, from all countries where the gospel is believed, and from lands where the truth is preached and God is owned, for you would see every now and then down on earth a dying bed, but upwards through the skies, mounting among the stars, another spirit shot upward to complete the constellations of the glorified. And as these bright ones, all redeemed by his sufferings, enter heaven, they bring to Christ fresh answers to that question, "Why have you forsaken me?" And if stooping from his throne in glory the Prince of life takes view of the sons of men who are lingering here, even in this present assembly, he will see tonight a vast number of us met together around this table. I hope most, if not all, of us redeemed by his blood and rejoicing in his salvation; and the Father points down to-night to this place, and to thousands of similar scenes where believers cluster around the table of fellowship with their Lord, and he seems to say to the Saviour, "There is my answer to your question, 'Why have you forsaken me?'"

Beloved, we shall have an answer to our question something like that. When we get to heaven, perhaps not until then, God will tell us why he forsook us. When I tossed upon my bed three months ago in weary pain that robbed me of my night's rest, and my day's rest too, I asked why it was I was there, but I have realized since the reason, for God helped me afterwards so to preach that many souls were ingathered. Often you will find that God deserts you that he may be with you after a nobler sort - hides the light that afterwards the light of seven suns at once may break in upon your spirit, and there you shall learn that it was for his glory that he left you, for his glory that he tried your faith. Only mind you stand to that. Still cry to him, and still call him God, and never complain, hut ask him why, and pursue his work still under all difficulties; so being like Christ on earth, you shall be like Christ above, as to the answer.

I cannot sit down without saying just this word. God will never forsake his people for ever. But as many of you as are not his people, if you have not believed in him, he will forsake you for ever, and for ever, and for ever; and if you ask, "Why have you forsaken me?" You will get your answer in the echo of your words, "You have forsaken me."

"How shall you escape if you neglect so great salvation?"[94] "Believe in the Lord Jesus Christ, and you shall be saved"[95] [96]

---

[94] Hebrews 2:3
[95] Acts 16:31
[96] Our Lord's Solemn Enquiry – Sermon delivered April 7th, 1872

33 – The Sign of True Humanity

After this, Jesus, knowing that all was now finished, said (to fulfil the Scripture), "I thirst."

(John 19:28 ESV)

Jesus said, "I thirst," and this is the complaint of a man. Our Lord is the Maker of the oceans: it is his hand that opens the bottles of heaven, and sends rain upon the evil and upon the good. "The sea is his, and he made it"[97] and all fountains and springs are of his digging. He pours out the streams that run among the hills, the torrents which rush adown the mountains, and the flowing rivers which enrich the plains.

One would have said, if he were thirsty he would not tell us, for all the clouds and rains would be glad to refresh his brow, and the brooks and streams would joyously flow at

---

[97] Psalm 95:5

his feet. And yet, though he was Lord of all, he had so fully taken upon himself the form of a servant and was so perfectly made in the likeness of sinful flesh, that he cried with fainting voice, "I thirst."

How truly man he is; he is, indeed, "bone of our bone and flesh of our flesh"[98] for he bears our infirmities. I invite you to meditate upon the true humanity of our Lord very reverently, and very lovingly. Jesus was proved to be really man, because he suffered the pains which belong to manhood. Angels cannot suffer thirst. A phantom, as some have called him, could not suffer in his fashion: but Jesus really suffered the pangs of flesh and blood.

Thirst is a common-place misery, which may happen to peasants or beggars; it is a real pain, and not a thing of a fancy or a nightmare of dreamland. Thirst is no royal grief, but an evil of universal manhood; Jesus is brother to the poorest and most humble of our race. Our Lord, however, endured thirst to an extreme degree, for it was the thirst of death which was upon him, and

---

[98] Genesis 2:23

more, it was the thirst of one whose death was not a common one, for "he tasted death for every man."[99]

It was pain that dried his mouth and made it like an oven, till he declared, in the language of the twenty-second psalm, "My tongue sticks to the roof of my mouth"[100] Believing this, let us tenderly feel how very near to us our Lord Jesus has become. You have been ill, and you have been parched with fever as he was, and then you too have gasped out "I thirst."

Your path runs hard by that of your Master. He said, "I thirst," in order that one might bring him drink, even as you have wished to have a cooling draught handed to you when you could not help yourself. Can you help feeling how very near Jesus is to us when his lips must be moistened with a sponge, and he must be so dependent upon others as to ask drink from their hand? Next time your fevered lips murmur "I am very thirsty," you may say to yourself, "Those are sacred words, for my Lord spoke in that fashion."

---

[99] Hebrews 2:9
[100] Psalm 22:15

Ah, beloved, our Lord was so truly man that all our griefs remind us of him: the next time we are thirsty we may gaze upon him; and whenever we see a friend faint and thirsting while dying we may behold our Lord dimly, but truly, mirrored in his members. How near the thirsty Saviour is to us; let us love him more and more.

Do not let us forget the infinite distance between the Lord of glory on his throne and the Crucified dried up with thirst. A river of the water of life, pure as crystal, flows today out of the throne of God and of the Lamb, and yet once he condescended to say, "I thirst," before his angelic guards, they would surely have emulated the courage of the men of David when they cut their way to the well of Bethlehem that was within the gate, and drew water in jeopardy of their lives. [101]

If Jesus said, "I thirst," then he knows all our frailties and woes. The next time we are in pain or are suffering depression of spirit we will remember that our Lord understands it all, for he has had practical, personal experience of it. Neither in torture of body

---

[101] 2 Samuel 23:16

nor in sadness of heart are we deserted by our Lord; his line is parallel with ours. The arrow which has lately pierced you, my brother, was first stained with his blood. The cup of which you are made to drink, though it be very bitter, bears the mark of his lips about its brim. He has traversed the mournful way before you, and every footprint you leave in the sodden soil is stamped side by side with his footmarks. Let the sympathy of Christ, then, be fully believed in and deeply appreciated, since he said, "I thirst."[102]

---

[102] The Shortest of the Seven Cries – Sermon delivered April 14th, 1878

34 – The Token of Suffering

After this, Jesus, knowing that all was now finished, said (to fulfil the Scripture), "I thirst."

(John 19:28 ESV)

The great Saviour says, "I thirst," because he is placed in the sinner's stead, and he must therefore undergo the penalty of sin for the ungodly. "My God, my God, why have you forsaken me?" points to the anguish of his soul; "I thirst" expresses in part the torture of his body; and they were both needed, because it is written of the God of justice that he is "able to destroy both soul and body in hell"[103] and the pangs that are due to law are of both kinds, touching both heart and flesh.

Our first parents plucked forbidden fruit, and by eating slew the race. Appetite was the

---

[103] Matthew 10:28

door of sin, and therefore in that point our Lord was put to pain. With "I thirst" the evil is destroyed and receives its expiation. I saw the other day the emblem of a serpent with its tail in its mouth, and if I carry it a little beyond the artist's intention the symbol may set forth appetite swallowing up itself. A carnal appetite of the body, the satisfaction of the desire for food, first brought us down under the first Adam, and now the pang of thirst, the denial of what the body craved for, restores us to our place.

We know from experience that the effect of sin in every man who indulges in it is thirst of soul. Thirst is dissatisfaction, the craving of the mind for something which it has not, but which it pines for. Our Lord says, "If any man thirst, let him come unto me and drink"[104] that thirst being the result of sin in every ungodly man at this moment. Now Christ standing in the stead of the ungodly suffers thirst as a type of his enduring the result of sin.

If Jesus had not thirsted, every one of us would have thirsted for ever far off from

---

[104] John 7:37

God, with an impassable gulf between us and heaven. Our sinful tongues, blistered by the fever of passion, must have burned for ever had not his tongue been tormented with thirst in our stead. I suppose that the "I thirst" was uttered softly, so that perhaps only one and another who stood near the cross heard it at all; in contrast with the louder cry of *"Lama sabachthani"* and the triumphant shout of "It is finished": but that soft, expiring sigh, "I thirst," has ended for us the thirst which else, insatiably fierce, had preyed upon us throughout eternity. Oh, wondrous substitution of the just for the unjust, of God for man, of the perfect Christ for us guilty, hell-deserving rebels. Let us magnify and bless our Redeemer's name.

It seems to me very wonderful that this "I thirst" should be, as it were, the clearance of it all. He had no sooner said "I thirst," and sipped the vinegar, than he shouted, "It is finished"; and all was over: the battle was fought and the victory won for ever, and our great Deliverer's thirst was the sign of his having defeated the last foe. The great agony of being forsaken by God was over, and he felt faint when the strain was withdrawn. I like to think of our Lord's saying, "It is finished," directly after he had exclaimed, "I thirst"; for these two voices come so naturally together.

Our glorious Samson had been fighting our foes; heaps upon heaps he had slain his thousands, and now like Samson he was sore athirst. He sipped of the vinegar, and he was refreshed, and no sooner has he thrown off the thirst than he shouted like a conqueror, "It is finished," and quitted the field, covered with renown. Let us exult as we see our Substitute going through with his work even to the bitter end, and then returning to his Father, God. O souls, burdened with sin, rest here and, in resting, live.[105]

---

[105] The Shortest of the Seven Cries – Sermon delivered April 14th, 1878

35 – Man's Treatment

After this, Jesus, knowing that all was now finished, said (to fulfil the Scripture), "I thirst."

(John 19:28 ESV)

According to modern thought man is a very fine and noble creature, struggling to become better. He is greatly to be commended and admired, for his sin is said to be seeking after God, and his superstition is a struggling after light.

Great and worshipful being that he is, truth is to be altered for him, the gospel is to be modulated to suit the tone of his various generations, and all the arrangements of the universe are to be rendered subservient to his interests. Justice must fly the field lest it be severe to so deserving a being; as for punishment, it must not be whispered to his polite ears.

In fact, the tendency is to exalt man above God and give him the highest place. But such is not the truthful estimate of man according to the Scriptures: there man is a fallen creature, with a carnal mind which cannot be reconciled to God; a worse than brutish creature, rendering evil for good, and treating his God with vile ingratitude. Alas, man is the slave and the dupe of Satan, and a black-hearted traitor to his God.

Did not the prophecies say that man would give to his incarnate God gall to eat and vinegar to drink? It is done. He came to save, and man denied him hospitality: at the first there was no room for him at the inn, and at the last there was not one cool cup of water for him to drink; but when he thirsted they gave him vinegar to drink.

This is man's treatment of his Saviour. Universal manhood, left to itself, rejects, crucifies, and mocks the Christ of God. This was the act too of man at his best, when he is moved to pity; for it seems clear that he who lifted up the wet sponge to the Redeemer's lips, did it in compassion. I think that Roman soldier meant well, at least well for a rough warrior with his little light and knowledge. He ran and filled a sponge with vinegar: it was the best way he knew of putting a few drops of moisture to the lips of one who was suffering so much; but though he felt a degree of pity, it was such as one might show to a dog; he felt no reverence, but mocked as he relieved. We read, "The soldiers also mocked him, offering him vinegar"[106]

When our Lord cried, "Eloi, Eloi," and afterwards said, "I thirst," the persons around the cross said, "Let be, let us see whether Elijah will come to save him"[107] mocking him; and, according to Mark, he who gave the vinegar uttered much the same words. He pitied the sufferer, but he thought so little of him that he joined in the voice of scorn.

See how man at his best mingles admiration of the Saviour's person with scorn of his claims; writing books to hold him up as an example and at the same moment rejecting his deity; admitting that he was a wonderful man, but denying his most sacred mission;

---

[106] Luke 23:36
[107] Matthew 27:39. Mark 15:36

extolling his ethical teaching and then trampling on his blood: thus giving him drink, but that drink vinegar. O my hearers, beware of praising Jesus and denying his atoning sacrifice. Beware of rendering him homage and dishonouring his name at the same time.

I cannot say much about man's cruelty to our Lord without touching myself and you. Have *we* not often given him vinegar to drink? Did we not do so years ago before we knew him? We used to melt when we heard about his sufferings, but we did not turn from our sins. We gave him our tears and then grieved him with our sins. We thought sometimes that we loved him as we heard the story of his death, but we did not change our lives for his sake, nor put our trust in him, and so we gave him vinegar to drink.

Nor does the grief end here, for have not the best works we have ever done, and the best feelings we ever felt, and the best prayers we have ever offered, been sour with sin? Can they be compared to generous wine? Are they not more like sharp vinegar? I wonder he has ever received them, as one marvels why he received this vinegar; and yet he has received them, and smiled upon us for presenting them. He knew once how to turn water into wine, and in matchless love he has often turned our sour drink-offerings into something sweet to himself, though in themselves, they have been the juice of sour grapes, sharp enough to set his teeth on edge. [108]

---

[108] The Shortest of the Seven Cries – Sermon delivered April 14th, 1878

36 – The Desire of His Heart

After this, Jesus, knowing that all was now finished, said (to fulfil the Scripture), "I thirst."

(John 19:28 ESV)

I cannot think that natural thirst was all he felt. He thirsted for water yes, but his soul was thirsty in a higher sense; indeed, he seems only to have spoken that the Scriptures might be fulfilled as to the offering him vinegar. He was always in harmony with himself, and his own body was always expressive of his soul's cravings as well as of its own longings.

"I thirst" meant that his heart was thirsting to save men. This thirst had been on him from the earliest of his earthly days. "Did you not know," said he, while still a boy, "that I must be about my Father's business?"[109] Did

---

[109] Luke 2:49

he not tell his disciples, "I have a baptism to be baptized with, and what constraint I am under until it is accomplished"[110]?

He thirsted to pluck us from between the jaws of hell, to pay our redemption price, and set us free from the eternal condemnation which hung over us; and when on the cross the work was almost done his thirst was not quenched, and could not be until he could say, "It is finished." It is almost done, you Christ of God; you have almost saved your people; there remains just one more thing, that you should actually die, and hence your strong desire to come to the end and complete your labour.

Beloved, there is now upon our Master, and there always has been, a thirst after the love of his people. Do you not remember how that thirst of his was strong in the old days of the prophet? Call to mind his complaint in the fifth chapter of Isaiah, "Now will I sing to my beloved a song of my beloved touching his vineyard. My beloved has a vineyard on a very fruitful hill: and he fenced it, and

---

[110] Luke 12:50

gathered out the stones, and planted it with the choicest vine, and built a tower in the midst of it, and also made a winepress."[111]

What was he looking for from his vineyard and its winepress? "And he looked that it should bring forth grapes, and it brought forth wild grapes"[112] — vinegar, and not wine; sourness, and not sweetness. So he was thirsting then.

According to the fifth chapter of the Song of Songs, we learn that when he drank in those olden times it was in the garden of his church that he was refreshed. "I have come into my garden, my sister, my spouse: I have gathered my myrrh with my spice; I have eaten my honeycomb with my honey; I have drunk my wine with my milk; eat, O friends; drink abundantly, O beloved."[113]

In the same song he speaks of his church, and says, "The roof of your mouth is as the best wine for my beloved, that goes down

---

[111] Isaiah 5:1-2

[112] Isaiah 5:2

[113] Song of Songs 5:1

sweetly, causing the lips of those that are asleep to speak."[114]

Yes, he loves to be with his people; they are the garden where he walks for refreshment, and their love, their graces, are the milk and wine which he delights to drink. Christ was always thirsty to save men, and to be loved of men; and we see a type of his life-long desire when, being weary, he sat on the well and said to the woman of Samaria, "Give me a drink."[115]

There was a deeper meaning in his words than she dreamed of, when he said to his disciples, "I have meat to eat that you know not of."[116] He derived spiritual refreshment from the winning of that women's heart to himself.

And now, our blessed Lord has a thirst for communion with each one of you who are his people, not because you can do him good, but because he can do you good. He thirsts to bless you and to receive your grateful love in return; he thirsts to see you

---

[114] Song of Songs 7:9
[115] John 4:7
[116] John 4:32

looking with believing eyes to his fullness, and holding out your emptiness that he may supply it. He says, "Behold, I stand at the door and knock."[117] What does he knock for? It is that he may eat and drink with you, for he promises that if we open to him he will enter in and eat with us and we with him.

And what makes him love us so? Ah, that I cannot tell, except his own great love. He *must* love, it is his nature. He must love his chosen whom he has once begun to love, for he is the same yesterday, to-day, and for ever.

His great love makes him thirst to have us much nearer than we are; he will never be satisfied till all his redeemed are beyond gunshot of the enemy.

He wants you brother, he wants you, dear sister, he longs to have you wholly to himself. Come to him in prayer, come to him in fellowship, come to him by perfect consecration, come to him by surrendering

---

[117] Revelation 3:20

your whole being to the sweet mysterious influences of his Spirit. [118]

---

[118] The Shortest of the Seven Cries – Sermon delivered April 14th, 1878

37 – Come to the Tomb

"Come, see the place where the Lord lay"

(Matthew 28:6 ESV)

Every circumstance connected with the life of Christ is deeply interesting to the Christian mind.

"His cross, his manger, and his crown, Are big with glories yet unknown."[119]

All his weary pilgrimage, from Bethlehem's manger to Calvary's cross, is, in our eyes, paved with glory. Each spot upon which he trod is to our souls consecrated, simply because there the foot of earth's Saviour and our own Redeemer once was placed. When he comes to Calvary, the interest thickens; then our best thoughts are centred on him in the agonies of crucifixion. Our deep affection does not permit us to leave him, even when, the struggle being over, he yields up the ghost.

---

[119] Unknown

His body, when it is taken down from the tree, still is lovely in our eyes. By faith we discern Joseph of Arimathea, and the timid Nicodemus, assisted by those holy women, drawing out the nails and taking down the mangled body; we behold them wrapping him in clean, white linen, girding him round with belts of spices; then putting him in his tomb, and departing for the Sabbath rest.

We shall, on this occasion, go where Mary went on the morning of the first day of the week, when waking from her couch before the dawn, she aroused herself to be early at the sepulchre of Jesus.

We will try, if it be possible, by the help of God's Spirit, to go as she did — we will stand at that tomb; we will examine it, and we trust we shall hear some truth-speaking voice coming from its hollow bosom which will comfort and instruct us.

Angels said, "Come, see the place where the Lord lay." The Syriac version reads, "Come, see the place where *our* Lord lay." Yes, angels put themselves with those poor women, and used one common pronoun —

our. Jesus is the Lord of angels as well as of men.

Fear not to enter that tomb. I will admit that catacombs are not the places where we, who are full of joy, would love to go. There is something gloomy about a vault. There are noxious smells of corruption; pestilence is born where a dead body has lain; but fear it not, Christian, for Christ was not left in hell neither did his body see corruption. Come, there is no scent, rather a perfume. No worms ever devoured his flesh; no rottenness ever entered into his bones; he saw no corruption.

Three days he slumbered, but no long enough to putrefy; he soon arose, perfect as when he entered, uninjured as when his limbs were composed for their slumber. Come then, Christian, summon up your thoughts, gather all your powers; here is a sweet invitation, let me press it again. Let me lead you by the hand of meditation, my brother; let me take you by the arm of your fancy, and let me again say to you, "Come, see the place where the Lord lay."

Oh! I have longed for rest, for I have heard

this world in my ears so long, that I have begged for a place where I might hide myself forever. I am sick of this tiring and trying life; my frame is weary, my soul is mad to repose herself awhile.

I wish I could lay myself down a little by the edge of some pebbly brook, with no companion except the fair flowers or the nodding willows. I would I could recline in stillness, where the air brings balm to the tormented brain, where there is no murmur except the hum of the summer bee, no whisper except that of the zephyrs, and no song except the carolling of the lark.

I wish I could be at ease for a moment. I have become a man of the world; my brain is racked, my soul is tired. Oh! Would you be quiet, Christian? Would you rest from your toils? Would you be calm for once? Then come here.

It is in a pleasant garden, far from the hum of Jerusalem; the noise and din of business will not reach you there; "Come, see the place where the Lord lay." It is a sweet resting spot, a withdrawing room for your soul, where you may brush from your

garments the dust of earth and muse awhile
in   peace.[120]

---

[120] The Tomb of Jesus – Sermon delivered April 8,
1855

38 – No Common Grave

"Come, see the place where the Lord lay"

(Matthew 28:6 ESV)

It is no common grave; it is not an excavation dug out by the spade for a pauper, in which to hide the last remains of his miserable and over-wearied bones. It is a princely tomb; it was made of marble, cut in the side of a hill. Stand here, believer, and ask why Jesus had such a costly sepulchre. He had no elegant garments; He owned no sumptuous palace, for he had not where to lay his head. His sandals were not rich with gold. He was poor.

Why, then does he lie in a noble grave? Christ was unhonoured till he had finished his sufferings; Christ's body suffered shame, spitting, buffeting, and reproach, until he had completed his great work; he was trampled underfoot, he was "despised and rejected of men; a man of sorrows, and acquainted with grief"[121] but the moment he had finished his undertaking, God said no more shall that body be disgraced.

Jesus, after he had finished his work, slept in a costly grave; for now his Father loved and honoured him, since his work was done.

Though it is a costly grave, *it is a borrowed one.* I see over the top of it, "Sacred to the memory of the family of Joseph of Arimathea" yet Jesus slept there. Yes, he was buried in another's tomb. He who had no house of his own, and rested in the habitation of other men. He had no table, but lived upon the hospitality of his disciples; who borrowed boats in which to preach, and had not anything in the wide world, was obliged to have a tomb from charity.

It was a borrowed tomb; and why? I take it to show that, as his sins were borrowed sins, so his burial was in a borrowed grave. Christ had no transgressions of his own; he took ours upon his head; he never committed a wrong, but he took all my sin, and all yours, if you are believers; concerning all his

---

[121] Isaiah 53:3

people, it is true, he bore their griefs and carried their sorrows in his own body on the tree; therefore, as they were others' sins, so he rested in another's grave; as they were sins imputed, so that grave was only imputedly his. It was not his tomb; it was the tomb of Joseph.

We have learned a little, then, with attention; but let us stoop down once more before we leave the grave, and notice something else. Why are the grave-clothes wrapped up? The Jews said robbers had abstracted the body; but if so, surely they would have stolen the clothes; they would never have thought of wrapping them up and laying them down so carefully; they would be too much in haste to think of it.

Why was it then? To manifest to us that Christ did not come out in a hurried manner. He slept till the last moment; then he awoke; he came not in haste. So at the precise hour, the decreed instant, Jesus Christ leisurely awoke, took off his garments, left them all behind him, and came forth

Pay attention to the tomb, your Jesus once lay there. He was a murdered man, my soul, and you the murderer.

"Ah, you my sins, my cruel sins,
His chief tormentors were,
Each of my crimes became a nail,
And unbelief the spear."
Alas! And did my Saviour bleed?
And did my Sovereign die?"[122]

My right hand struck the dagger to his heart. My deeds killed Christ. Alas! I killed him who loved me with an everlasting love. Eyes, why do you refuse to weep when you see Jesus' body mangled and torn? Oh! Give vent to your sorrow, Christians, for you have good reason to do so. It seemed so sad a thing that Christ should have to die; and to me it often appears too great a price for Jesus Christ to purchase worms with his own blood.

It seems too costly for him who is the Prince of Life and Glory to let his fair limbs be tortured in agony; that the hands which carried mercies should be pierced with accursed nails; that the temples that were always clothed with love should have cruel

---

[122] Alas! And did my Savior bleed. Isaac Watts

thorns driven through them. It appears too much. Oh! Weep, Christian, and let your sorrow rise. Is not the price all but too great, that your beloved should for you resign *himself?* Oh! I should think, if a person were saved from death by another, he would always feel deep grief if his deliverer lost his life in the attempt. I had a friend, who, standing by the side of a piece of frozen water, saw a young lad in it, and sprang upon the ice in order to save him. After clutching the boy, he held him in his hands and cried out, "Here he is! Here he is! I have saved him." But, just as they caught hold of the boy, he sank himself, and his body was not found for some time afterwards, when he was dead. Oh! It is so with Jesus. My soul was drowning. From heaven's high portals he saw me sinking in the depths of hell; he plunged in:

"He sank beneath his heavy woes, To raise me to a crown; There's ne'er a gift his hand bestows, But cost his heart a groan."[123] [124]

---

[123] Unknown

[124] The Tomb of Jesus – Sermon delivered April 8, 1855

39 – Joy and Gladness

"Come, see the place where the Lord lay"
(Matthew 28:6 ESV)

"Come, see the place where the Lord
lay." *with solemn awe* for you and I will
have to lie there too.
"Hark! From the tomb a doleful sound,
Mine ears, attend the cry,
You living men, come view the ground
Where you must shortly lie."

"Princes, this clay must be your bed,
In spite of all your powers.
The tall, the wise, the reverend head,
Must lie as low as ours."[125]

It is a fact we do not often think of, that we
shall all be dead in a little while.

---

[125] Hark! From the tomb, Isaac Watts

I know that I am made of dust, and not of iron; in a little while my body must crumble back to its native elements. But do you ever try to picture to yourself the moment of your dissolution? My friends, there are some of you who seldom realize how old you are, how near you are to death. We should remember our frailty.

Sometimes I have tried to think of the time of my departure. I do not know whether I shall die a violent death or not; but I would ask God that I might die suddenly; for sudden death is sudden glory. But it is not mine to choose. Suppose I lie lingering for weeks, in the midst of pains, and griefs, and agonies; when that moment comes, that moment which is too solemn for my lips to speak of, when the spirit leaves the clay — when that moment comes, O you lips, be dumb, and profane not its solemnity. When death comes, how is the strong man bowed down! How the mighty man falls! They may say they will not die, but there is no hope for them; they must yield, the arrow has gone home.

I knew a man who was a wicked wretch, and I remember seeing him pace the floor of his bedroom saying "O God, I will not die, I will not die." When I begged him to lie on his bed, for he was dying, he said he could not die while he could walk, and he would walk till he did die. He expired in the utmost torments, always shrieking, "O God, I will not die." Oh! That moment, that last moment. See how clammy is the sweat upon the brow, how dry the tongue, how parched the lips. The man shuts his eyes and slumbers, then opens them again, if he be a Christian.

We can scarcely say, "He is gone," before the ransomed spirit takes its mansion near the throne. Come to Christ's tomb, then, for the silent vault must soon be your habitation. Come to Christ's grave, for you must slumber there.

"Come, see the place where the Lord lay," *with joy and gladness.*

He does not lie there now.

Weep, when you see the tomb of Christ, but rejoice because it is empty. Your sin killed him, but his divinity raised him up. Your guilt murdered him, but his righteousness restored him.

Oh! He has burst the bonds of death, and has come out more than conqueror, crushing death beneath his feet. Rejoice, O Christian, for he is not there—he is risen.[126]

---

[126] The Tomb of Jesus – Sermon delivered April 8, 1855

40 – Our Future

"Come, see the place where the Lord lay"
(Matthew 28:6 ESV)

The first thing you perceive, if you stand by his empty tomb, is *his divinity*. The dead in Christ shall rise first at the resurrection: but he who rose first—their leader, rose in a different fashion. They rise by imparted power. He rose by his own.

He could not slumber in the grave, because he was God. Death had no more dominion over him. There is no better proof of Christ's divinity that that startling resurrection of his, when he rose from the grave, by the glory of the Father. O Christian, your Jesus is a God; his broad shoulders that hold you up are indeed divine; and here you have the best proof of it—because he rose from the grave.

Behold his empty tomb, O true believer: it is a sign of *your acquittal*, and your full discharge. If Jesus had not paid the debt, he would not have risen from the grave. He would have lain there till this moment if he had not cancelled the entire debt, by satisfying eternal vengeance.

O beloved, is not that an overwhelming thought?

> "It is finished, it is finished,
> Hear the rising Saviour cry."[127]

As a justified man, I have not a sin now against me in God's book. If I were to turn over God's eternal book, I should see every debt of mine receipted and cancelled.

"Here's pardon for transgressions past,
It matter not how black their cast,
And O my soul, with wonder view,
For sins to come, here's pardon too.
Fully discharged by Christ I am,
From Christ's tremendous curse and blame."[128]

Jesus rose, and as the Lord our Saviour rose, so all his followers must rise. Die I must—this body must be a carnival for worms; the

---

[127] Hark the voice of love and mercy, Jonathan Evans and Benjamin Francis
[128] O that I had seraph's fire, John Kent

constituent particles of my frame will enter into plants, from plants pass into animals, and thus be carried into far distant realms; but, at the blast of the archangel's trumpet, every separate atom of my body shall find its fellow; like the bones lying in the valley of vision, though separated from one another, the moment God shall speak, the bone will creep to its bone; then the flesh shall come upon it; the four winds of heaven shall blow, and the breath shall return.

So let me die, let beasts devour me, let fire turn this body into gas and vapour, all its particles shall yet again be restored; this very self-same, actual body shall stare up from its grave, glorified and made like Christ's body, yet still the same body, for God has said it. Christ's same body rose; so shall mine.

O my soul, dost you now dread to die? You will lose your partner body a little while, but you will be married again in heaven; soul and body shall again be united before the throne of God. The grave — what is it? It is the bath in which the Christian puts the clothes of his body to have them washed and cleansed. Death—what is it? It is the waiting-room where we robe ourselves for immortality; it is the place where the body, like Esther, bathes itself in spices that it may be fit for the embrace of its Lord. Death is the gate of life; I will not fear to die, then, but will say,

> "Shudder not to pass the stream;
> Venture all your care on him;
> Him whose dying love and power
> Stilled its tossing, hushed its roar,
> Safe in the expanded wave;
> Gentle as a summer's eve.
> Not one object of his care
> Ever suffered shipwreck there."[129]

Come, view the place then, where the Lord lay. Go to Christ's grave, both to weep and to rejoice. [130]

---

[129] The dying believer to his soul, Augustus Toplady
[130] The Tomb of Jesus – Sermon delivered April 8, 1855

Enjoyed this book? Please leave a review on Amazon

For a free ebook, more resources to help everybody apply the good news of Jesus to everyday life, and to be the first to hear about our latest releases and special offers, visit justworshipgod.com

Find us everywhere on social media @justworshipgod

Made in the USA
Monee, IL
27 March 2022

93636819R00121